LETTING GO

HOW A FAMILY CRISIS BROUGHT CLARITY AND AUTHENTICITY

Lisa Hoelzer

ISBN: 979-8-9888225-0-9 (Paperback)

ISBN: 979-8-9888225-1-6 (Hardcover)

ISBN: 979-8-9888225-2-3 (e-book)

Library of Congress Control Number: 2023914658

This book is memoir. It reflects the author's present recollections of experiences over time. Some names and characteristics have been changed, some events have been compressed, and some dialogue has been recreated.

Printed by Navy Blue Press, in Provo, Utah, USA.

First printing, 2023.

CONTENTS

PROLOGUE

When I got home from the church meeting, the kids were already in bed. My husband, Bryan, would have attended with me, but we couldn't find a babysitter. He didn't mind staying home, though. He was the resident anesthesiologist for a complicated surgery being performed the next day and had to study for the case. He'd be in trouble with his attending if he didn't prepare adequately.

"How was it?" Bryan asked, as we hugged in greeting.

"Pretty much the usual," I responded, adjusting my skirt as we sat down to talk. "It was surprisingly full for an evening meeting. Mostly couples, which is typical, but a few lone singles like me. One guy came in a polo shirt! I guess he didn't get the memo that it was Sunday dress. How were the kids?"

"They were great!" Bryan's positivity and cheery nature was one of the many things that made me fall in love with him.

"That's good. There was one speaker tonight that I'm still thinking about. He talked about in-group favoritism, which I learned about in social psychology. Remember how much I loved that class? He explained how research shows that every group thinks they are a little bit better than other groups—a little more honest, a little more generous, a little more righteous. I don't remember his actual point. He must have been telling us to avoid this bias and love all people, whether a part of the church or not. But I thought, 'How could members of our church possibly overcome this belief?' I mean, we literally teach that we are the only true church on the earth." I jokingly added, "Of course we're better than people not in our church! We get to go to heaven, and they don't, simple as that."

"But," Bryan interjected, "we believe that anyone can learn about our doctrine and join the church. That's why we send nineteen-year-olds on missions and why we're always told to talk to our neighbors about the church."

"That's true. But that part gets me too. We think everyone in the world should be like us—not only embrace our doctrine, but dress, act, and relate to each other as we do. Even when people do convert, we have a hard time accepting them unless they look and behave a certain way. *Then* they can be part of the 'chosen' crowd."

"I know, that is troubling. But the church has so much good to offer, too. It's great for our family."

I agreed that we had benefited from our membership in the church. We had a wonderful sense of community. Everywhere we moved, we had instant friends once we attended church. The members care about and support each other. The church helped us hold our kids to high standards of behavior, including modesty and service to others. We believed in the doctrine and wanted to be obedient so that we could live with our family in heaven for all eternity.

However, part of me was skeptical. That fascinating social psychology class had taught me that as researchers study human behavior, patterns emerge. By gathering large amounts of data, they discover that even though individuals think they are acting in ways unique and personal to their situation, often they are following trends and repeating configurations, many of which have been around for millennia. Some of these ways of interacting are so common that they have been named. Examples include the bystander effect, confirmation bias, and diffusion of responsibility. In-group favoritism is another example. The tendency to make favorable, positive attributions to behaviors by members of our in-group, and unfavorable, negative attributions to behaviors by members of out-groups is a universal occurrence; the tighter and more homogenous the group, the stronger this bias shows up. How do we know our church really is the best and has all the truth? Maybe we are as susceptible to bias as any other group.

Over the years, my skepticism had grown as I had more life experience, read books, and talked to people from different places. Discovering how wide the world is had made me realize there are many ways of living and many ideas about the right and wrong ways to live. We're not the only ones who think that our way is the best way. I wanted to stay true to my church, and I did feel that was the best path for my family, but deep down I was bothered by the arrogance and ethnocentricity inherent in believing that of all the people on the earth today (not to mention all who ever have or will live), the people in *our* group are the only ones who get to know the truth and be saved.

Bryan had heard my thoughts on this topic before, and we didn't have time to discuss them in depth tonight. We chatted for a few more minutes and then headed to bed.

CHAPTER 1

Searching for Help

I opened the hall closet door and called out to Bryan, "I'll pack the towels." As I contemplated how many and which ones to take, I received a text from my daughter Brooke.

> hey mom i'm sorry i'm texting you about this instead of talking to you I just don't know how to get these words out. also i'm really only telling you this out of necessity, partly because being in a swimsuit at lake powell will expose some things and partly because everything seems so bad and it's not getting better. but basically i'm always just really really sad and miserable or completely numb and don't care abt anything and bc of this I think abt how I

> want to die or just not be living constantly, and i've recently had an unhealthy coping mechanism of hurting myself which is what you might notice when i'm in a swimsuit. it's not a big deal i've been surviving through this but it feels like a lot more than just normal teenage emotions. i'm so sorry.

My breathing stopped as my throat constricted. At the same time, my body felt calm and slow. I walked to my bedroom and sank into one of the armchairs in a daze. Is this for real? How could it be this bad and I didn't even know? I quickly thought through the rest of the day. It was 9:47 a.m., August 26, 2020. We were packing for a trip to Lake Powell and hoping to leave around one thirty p.m., after the girls got home from school. Like everyone else in the world, many of our trips had been canceled this year. We were thankful to be able to squeeze in a quick trip to the lake, a place we felt safe from Covid because we'd be far apart from other boaters and out in the open air where viruses are blown away by the wind.

Our oversized master bedroom had an alcove by the window with two chairs and a small table. Bryan and I sat there and talked often. The large window had a beautiful view of the mountains to the north and east. Our home was new and modern with white trim and walls painted a soothing color aptly named Agreeable Gray. I felt the humid heat from the bathroom where Bryan and I had each recently showered, intertwined with the cool breeze from the fan attached to the vaulted ceiling. I stared blankly out the window, trying to process this news from Brooke.

While this news was devastating, I knew that if any parent could handle a situation like this, I could. I studied clinical therapy in graduate school and had continued to read and analyze books and articles related to mental health. Working through my own emotional challenges in the past few years led me to concepts and answers that had changed my life. Additionally, as a stay-at-home mom, I had ample time to research treatment options, take my kids to appointments, refill their prescriptions, and spend quality one-on-one time with them. My organizational skills allowed me to manage my time and the household tasks with efficiency and continue to carve out time for my own self-care.

My mind flitted back to scenes over the past year: Brooke more and more withdrawn, hanging out in her room or on the couch, crouched over her phone. I had noticed this change but attributed it to normal teenage moodiness. We had two older daughters, Kaitlin and Haley, who had gone through similar patterns. At fifteen and sixteen they had been less interested in family activities, grumpier with us in conversation, and spent more time alone with their phones. With Kaitlin, the oldest, we worried a lot. We thought she might be like this the rest of her life. We pictured tense interactions and strained conversations ad infinitum. But no; she got older and more mature and came back into herself. Haley had a similar pattern. Around eighteen years old they both became friendlier and more helpful around the house. They went off to college, and in our experience, during that year they became not only nice, but also grateful and complimentary. We have a strong, enjoyable relationship with both our older daughters.

Brooke was sixteen and had begun her junior year of high school two weeks before. I had been somewhat worried about her in the past few months, but she hadn't said anything about feeling bad, so I chalked it up to these melancholic teenage years.

My mind reeled with this sudden news. Sweet, darling Brooke? She was the easiest, most cooperative child, full of joy and enthusiasm for life. She was happy, pleasant, and fun to be around as she grew up, a pure delight to parent. As a three-year-old she made a game of giving us compliments. If Bryan or I said to her, "You're so sweet," she'd say back, "*You're* so sweet." We would continue, "You're so darling," ("*You're* so darling") for as many positive attributes we could think of. It was a game that made you feel so good you wanted to keep playing as long as possible.

Brooke never had a temper tantrum that I can remember. If she wanted something that we wouldn't allow her to have, we could easily assuage her frustration. I could say, "We'll talk about it later," or, "Tomorrow we get to go there," and she would reply, "Okay," and be over it. She always tried to do what was right and what we wanted her to do. She enjoyed pleasing us and other adults.

One time when Brooke was seven, a friend of mine was watching our kids while Bryan and I went on vacation. She got a kick out of Brooke's enthusiasm and *joie de vivre.* My friend and her husband were in the kitchen, and Brooke came running in from playing outside. "There's a bird's nest in the playset!" she exclaimed with great delight. Then she added, "This is the best day of my life!" My friend was greatly amused.

Brooke did her homework and chores without a fuss. She was nice to her younger sister, Sydney, even when Sydney was cranky or unkind to her. She enjoyed our family activities and found the good in every situation. It was hard to imagine or believe that she felt this depressed. It broke my heart to think of her hurting. I was equally devastated that she hadn't told me before this (and only now told me because I might see scabs or scars on her skin). My heart hurt to read how apologetic she was, as if she was a problem or troubling me.

Bryan walked into the room and my mind snapped back to the present. He could tell something was wrong and walked toward me with a questioning look. I handed him the phone and he sat in the chair beside me as he read. He had a pained expression on his face. He looked up and asked, "What are we going to do?"

I wanted to reply to Brooke quickly to alleviate her wondering and distress over the confession. I told Bryan, "I'll go up to the school and talk to her. I want to discuss this in person before we leave on the trip."

I texted Brooke back: "Oh, honey, I'm so sorry. I'm so glad you told me though. I am going to come up to the school to talk more about this. I'll pull up next to your car and you can get in mine."

She agreed, and I drove quickly to the high school. Thankfully, it was only five minutes from our house. On the way, I thought through what I wanted to say and what the next steps would be. I have a special talent of staying calm in times of trauma or stress; this characteristic has served me well as a parent. Sometimes I refer to myself as an "under-reactor"—opposite of an overreactor. I felt this calm now, a comforting feeling that this would all work out. But, of course, I wanted to reassure Brooke that we were glad she told us and that we would get help for her.

This was not the first time one of our children needed help

with her mental health. When Kaitlin was a junior, she had a lot of anxiety. We could tell how frequently she didn't feel well, especially on school mornings. She threw up often and complained of shallow, strained breathing and a racing heartbeat. She had to get up at five thirty a.m. for an early-morning religion class that was part of the youth program in our church. She was committed to going and completing the four-year course of study, but it was a huge strain on her mental health.

To address Kaitlin's anxiety, we made appointments with our family's pediatrician and then with the counselor he recommended. She went to therapy and eventually got on medication. By her senior year she felt better. Since that time, we had moved to a different state, so we would need to find new providers for Brooke. We hadn't even been to a family doctor or pediatrician yet in our new area. Thankfully, we don't have any chronic health conditions, and nothing medical (or mental) had come up since we'd moved.

There was an open spot next to Brooke's car in the high school parking lot. I pulled in and saw Brooke sitting in her car. The red brick façade of the high school showed that it was more than fifty years old, and I knew the inside structure was even worse. The foundation hadn't been properly secured for the sloping ground it was built on, and the school was sliding almost imperceptibly toward the west, away from the mountains. The movement became obvious when pieces of cinder block fell from the tops of the walls, adjacent to the ceiling, onto the floor below. Luckily, no students had been hurt. Since that time, the building had been evaluated and deemed in need of rebuilding, or at least fortifying the foundation. The fight was on year after year to pass a bond to get the funding to complete the project.

Brooke got out of her car, and I got out also. I walked over to her and gave her a hug. I had tears in my eyes and in my voice as I told her, "I love you. I'm so sorry you've been going through this." I walked around the car, and we got in our respective seats. I said, "How come you haven't told me before this?" Of course, there's no good answer to this question, but I wanted to say it to let her know I wish she would have and that I would've been supportive and ready to help.

"I don't know. I didn't know how to say it."

"Well, I'm glad you've told me now. We will get you help; things will get better. I promise."

I asked her how long she'd been feeling like this. She said it began her sophomore year and slowly got worse. I thought back to how her grades had slipped a little last semester, at the end of her sophomore year. Brooke had earned straight A's up until then and had always been in the gifted programs and accelerated classes. I knew that declining grades was a sign of distress for adolescent students but going slightly down from constant 4.0's was understandable.

In the car, she told me she was often stressed about school. Her goal was a 4.0 each semester, but she was finding it harder and harder to accomplish that. Both her older sisters graduated high school with 4.0's—they *never* got anything less than an A. Brooke felt pressure to follow that example; she felt like that was the family expectation. And lately she had trouble concentrating. When she started her homework, she felt tired and sluggish, or, at other times, distracted and too energetic to sit still. She had more and more incomplete and missing assignments and that multiplied the stress.

I told her she does not need to get straight A's. In fact, I would appreciate it if she didn't because that would reduce the pressure on Sydney, the last of our four daughters. I said it is time to stop that trend and expectation. She was relieved by that, but I knew that wouldn't be the cure-all. There were other factors to her depression and telling someone "Don't worry about it" doesn't make the worry go away.

I said that I had noticed her distress in the past months and wasn't sure what to make of it. I'd seen her listless movements, flat affect, and disinterest in her usual activities. I still believed these could be explained by general adolescent malaise, but now I saw them as a list of symptoms of depression. I told her again that we'd get her the help she needed. I'd make appointments with the doctor to talk about medication and with some therapists to find one she connected with.

It was a hot day, and I had left the air conditioning running, but even then, the sun was beating down on our legs. We were running out of time because Brooke needed to get back to her last class of the day, but I had one more thing to ask while I had her in-person and alone.

"You said in your text that I would see something when you were in a swimsuit. I assume you're talking about places you have cut?"

She looked in her lap and nodded her head.

I nudged her, "Tell me more about that. When did it start and how often?"

"I've done it a few times over the summer, not that often though."

"Where are the cuts and are they healed by now?"

"Yeah, they're healed. They're on the tops of my thighs."

I didn't know what else to say. We'd never dealt with this problem before, although I was aware that some people used this as a coping method. I didn't want to overreact and scare her off from talking to me further (and overreacting is not my nature, anyway).

I said, "Well, we can talk about that more in the future. I know self-harm can ease emotional pain sometimes, but I hope we can find better ways for you to cope. I'm glad you told me about it. I'm sorry you're going through this. I know it's painful and hard. We love you and we want you to be able to feel better. We will do everything we can to help make that happen."

There were tears in both of our eyes as I reached over and hugged her again. I said she should get back to school and I would get back home to pack and prepare for our trip. I got out of the car when she got out and gave her another big hug. I watched her walk back into the school and wondered what our futures held.

Many families from our area vacation at Lake Powell. Most of them have part-ownership in a houseboat and own their own speedboat. They load up their food and supplies, drive the houseboat from the marina, and anchor it somewhere along the thousands of miles of shoreline on the borders of the lake for a week or more. The "lake" is actually a reservoir; a dam at one end controls the level of water that fills the giant canyon. There are seemingly innumerable coves, bays, and sandy slopes on which to anchor your houseboat.

Anywhere you stop, you are surrounded by sheer cliffs and giant walls of beautiful red sandstone. A vacation there is filled with adventurous water sports (wake surfing, water skiing, jet skiing, tubing, and hydra-foiling) as well as awe-inspiring views of nature.

We did not have any ownership in a houseboat, and although we could have rented one, we decided to go another route. We stayed at the hotel at the marina and rented a speed boat and the necessary water sports equipment for the four days we'd be there. There are advantages to this method: you don't have to pack your food and equipment onto the houseboat, you get to go out to eat every night instead of cooking and cleaning after each meal, and it costs a lot less. The downsides are that you drive your speedboat out and in from the marina each day, which is not as picturesque as the coves where you could anchor, and that everyone in your party must be out on the speedboat all day together. You can come in to drop off or pick up different members at the marina, but that takes extra time. When you have a houseboat, the speedboat makes multiple trips during the day and picks up and drops off those who want to go in or out. We decided to do the hotel route this time to try out Lake Powell and see what we thought and then decide if we wanted to rent a houseboat in the future.

There was one distinct advantage to having a hotel on this trip, however. When you go out to the far regions of the lake to find a secluded spot to anchor your houseboat, you lose cell service. I needed cell service to make appointments for Brooke as soon as possible. I did not want to waste any time.

The marina hotel was not fancy but was well kept. In the

mornings, I walked up and down the hallway, tracking the patterns of the carpet with my eyes, as I made call after call in search of a therapist. I wanted Brooke to be assessed by a therapist before seeing a doctor about possible medications. But finding a therapist is not an easy task. A google search results in an overwhelming number of choices. How do you know which one will be a good fit? Many of the websites have pictures, which helps. But it's still a guess and a gamble. I didn't realize until later that you should also filter down your choices based on which clinics accept your insurance.

Many of the clinics I called had long wait lists for their providers. Rates of depression, anxiety, and suicide had gone up in recent months. Mental health professionals have been swamped ever since the pandemic started. The lack of social interaction, coupled with isolation at home—which can either be lonely or difficult on your relationships, depending on the size of your family—had strained many people's mental health.

I wanted to make appointments with several different therapists so Brooke could try them out and find the right one. When Bryan and I discussed our plan for Brooke's treatment on the five-hour drive to the lake, he told me about a prominent football player from his favorite team who had recently spoken publicly about his depression and anxiety. The player said that he had to see many therapists to find the right one for him. On average, a client sees four counselors before finding one he or she feels comfortable with. This is why it took many calls to accomplish my task.

Another daunting factor in this process was that clinics were mostly doing therapy over Zoom. This was not ideal. It is hard enough to meet a new therapist and talk about your troubles, but add in bad connections and delayed sound, and it can be discouraging. It's challenging to feel a connection to your therapist, or anyone, when you only see a grainy image of her face on a small screen. Also, it's hard to find privacy for a therapy session at home with your family around. But this was our only option. We could only hope that soon the virus would go away, or the vaccine would be ready, and therapists could accept clients into their offices once again.

I scoured the internet, made lists, made calls, crossed places off, made appointments. By the end of the trip, I had lined up three different counselors for Brooke to try and had set an appointment with an additional one who was three months booked out. As I wore out the carpet of the hotel hallway, I kept thinking how grateful I was to not be stuck far out on the lake with no cell service.

In between this research and list-making, I joined the family out on the boat every day. We took snacks and drinks and roamed the lake from morning until dinner time. There were eight of us on the boat: Bryan and me; Kaitlin and her husband of one and a half years Ben; Haley and her best friend Amanda; and Brooke and Sydney. Amanda and Haley roomed together their freshman year and had spent most of the summer together in Atlanta, Georgia, living with Amanda's family. They needed to work and earn money for college, but the only job they could find was "summer sales." They went door-to-door selling pest control. It was miserable, but they earned decent money. The difficulties of the summer made them extra grateful to be on vacation.

Out on the lake we took turns water skiing and wake surfing. When our four daughters are together, you can tell they are sisters. They are all tall and slender, they all have dark brown eyes, and their faces have the same contours. Brooke and Kaitlin look the most alike, with the same body shape and sandy-blonde hair. They are similar in personality also. As Brooke grew up, we marveled at how she did things like Kaitlin, from constant reading to the way they skied.

Haley is the only brunette. She has a slightly darker complexion than the rest and tans easily. At this point in the summer, she was a dark brown while the other three were pinkish white. Sydney's hair is lighter and straighter than her sisters'. At thirteen, she was already tall and on track to be the tallest of the four girls. Kaitlin and Ben looked a lot alike too, as many married couples do. They are about the same height and have the same color hair. They have a lot of traits in common: they are both smart and hard-working academically, and both are interesting and fun to talk to, with great senses of humor. Ben has been an excellent fit with our family from the start. The more comfortable he gets around us, the more we get to see his enjoyable and amusing personality come out.

Amanda has white-blonde hair and is medium height. She is so easy-going and fun to be around that she feels like one of the family, even though she doesn't look like a sister. In Atlanta, Amanda's family owns a speedboat and loves going to the lake as often as possible. When Haley and Amanda lived there over the summer, they went boating almost every weekend. Because of that, Haley and Amanda were the most skilled wake surfers. They could let go of the rope and surf for a long time, and they could move the board purposely up and down the wake and even do 180-degree turns. The rest of us were impressed and some of us tried to learn these tricks from them. We stopped for swim breaks often and did some cliff diving. Sometimes we just drove around, up and down the narrow canyons, appreciating the beauty of our surroundings.

Bryan and I did not have much time to talk during the trip. We were out on the boat with everyone most of the day, or I was inside making phone calls. In the evening, we went to dinner and hung out and talked together, and Sydney slept in the other bed in our hotel room. Luckily, we had the long drive there and back to talk things over while the girls had their earbuds in and couldn't overhear us.

It is not unusual for me and Bryan to talk for hours. We were best friends before we dated, and as friends, we would hang out together or talk on the phone, discussing our lives and our families, our thoughts about the future and the past. Bryan's mom observed this and knew we were meant for each other. Most nights of our married life, we spend an hour or two, sometimes more, reviewing our day and what was coming up that week. When we go on long hikes together or on trips, we get into deeper topics like life plans and changes, in-depth assessments of each of our children, or ideas we've been reading about or mulling over. This part of our relationship is deeply satisfying and keeps us emotionally close.

The drive from the lake back to our house is an easy one, mostly on major highways. I drove, and Bryan and I talked about the appointments I had made and what we thought the future would bring. We were both familiar with counseling, but not necessarily because we had participated in it. I have a master's in social work, a clinical program that trains you to be a therapist. I worked for less than a year before I had Kaitlin, and then we moved to a different state for Bryan to attend medical school. I haven't worked since then, but I read constantly, mostly nonfiction, on different topics, including self-help, parenting, and other psychology/counseling genres. I went to counseling briefly as an adult after my parents got a divorce. I didn't find it particularly helpful, but I didn't like my therapist and didn't have the funds or know-how to try to find one I did like.

Besides fulfilling his pre-med classes, Bryan's undergraduate major was human development. He had courses on parenting, marriage and relationship enrichment, and family life. He learned about the psychological and sociological development of humans and how to address problems in either area. In medical school he studied the DSM (the diagnostic manual for therapeutic clinicians, detailing the symptoms and diagnostic criteria for psychological problems), as well as the psychosocial aspects of medical problems. He also completed a psychiatry rotation in his fourth year of medical school.

Through our knowledge and experience, we had some idea of what this path would look like. We had read and heard about other families with teenagers struggling with depression. It was common and only getting more frequent. We knew Brooke would go to therapy and hoped she would find a counselor she liked and who was helpful. She would probably get on medication and that medication would take a while to work. We were aware that the risk of suicide attempt went up during the first weeks of taking an antidepressant. If Brooke's problem escalated, we understood generally how the system works and how to access more in-depth programs. We were heartbroken for Brooke and hated seeing her in pain. We weren't thrilled to be dealing with this problem, of course, but we felt lucky that we had knowledge of, and exposure to, the dynamics of mental health problems and treatments. We were ready to handle this, one day at a time.

Postscript: I never saw any marks on Brooke's legs on that trip. Later, when I looked closely, I could see the faint lines. She had not cut deeply, and the cuts were mostly healed. They will not leave scars. I'm glad Brooke thought I would see them, though. I'm relieved and grateful we planned that trip and it propelled her to tell us about her pain.

CHAPTER 2

The Making and Breaking of the Dream

In my junior year of high school, I was known as one of the smartest students in the school. My fellow students knew I got straight A's, aced AP tests, loved chemistry, and excelled in math. I worked hard but loved the work. I truly enjoyed learning. It was no surprise then that in the spring of that year, I was going to the math fair. It was a surprise, however, when a sophomore boy called me with a question about it. The math fair was held at a local university; students from surrounding high schools traveled there to compete against each other in a variety of categories. My now-husband, Bryan, called me the night before the fair to ask something—I can't remember what—and we ended up talking for more than thirty minutes. I can still picture where I sat during that conversation. Our kitchen had a built-in desk area next to the pantry, with the phone mounted to the wall on the right, about shoulder-height. As we talked, I sat on the desk, my feet on the chair, holding the yellow phone against my ear, and wrapping the cord around my fingers. I can see the gray raised-keypad of that phone, and I remember dialing Bryan's number from it many times over the next few years.

We hung out together at the math fair the next day, with other students from our high school, and we became friends after that. We talked in school and had some friends in common. That fall, when I was a senior, I hosted a surprise party at my house for one of my close friends. It was after a basketball game, and I anticipated a big crowd. I invited Bryan (now a junior) and his friends to come; many of the guys in his circle knew my friends. After that, our two groups hung out together the rest of my senior year. We went mini golfing, had barbecues, and ditched school to go out to breakfast. Sometimes two people in the group would pair off and date exclusively, but mostly we were simply good friends having fun.

Toward the end of my senior year, I dated someone from the group, but it was not Bryan. His name was Mark. After I asked him to a girls' choice dance, we went out together more and more often. I liked Mark a lot. He was quirky and witty. We doubled often with another fun couple from the group. Meanwhile, Bryan and I remained good friends. He was taller than me, had dark brown wavy hair, and was in good shape from being on the swim team. We got along easily and had a great time talking together. Bryan came over to my house after his lifeguard shifts and we'd chat and get pizza. A few times over the summer, Bryan asked a girl out, and he and I, not he and Mark, planned the double dates. I loved talking to Bryan and felt comfortable with him. I enjoyed going out with Mark, but I knew our relationship probably wouldn't last forever.

At the end of the summer, I went to a college in a different state. Mark and I broke up before I left, but I continued talking on the phone and writing letters to Bryan. Our long-distance bills were quite expensive. When his mom saw how well we got along and how long we could talk, she said, "You're going to marry that girl someday!" By the time I came home for Christmas break, we both knew we had feelings for each other and wanted to date. We continued our long-distance relationship over the next semester until I came home for the summer, and that's when things started to disintegrate.

Bryan was enjoying the end of his senior year and the related social activities. I selfishly felt hurt by his involvement with his friends and thought he should be spending more time with me. But the real problem was the cognitive dissonance between our values and our actions. Bryan and I were both quite religious. We belonged to the same conservative Christian denomination, and we had high standards for ourselves. We read our scriptures every day and prayed in the morning, at night, and over meals. We attended church on Sundays and tried our best to be honest, hardworking, and chaste. It was with the last quality that we ran into trouble. We were enormously in love and had the strong hormones of any healthy young adult. We believed in abstinence before marriage and thought that approach would set up a strong and loving union. However, we found it harder and harder to stick to the standards we wanted for ourselves and each other, and that resulted in arguments and hard feelings. We vacillated between blaming ourselves and blaming each other. There were a lot of despondent feelings and heartbreaking conversations.

Bryan's parents were active in our religion and supported him in his standards and values. We knew they wanted us to follow certain rules, and yet they didn't micromanage Bryan's activities and interactions. My parents, on the other hand, had stopped going to church as teenagers. They expected responsible, respectful behavior from their children, including earning good grades, completing household chores, and attending family activities. They provided a loving and stable home, but religion wasn't a part of it. This was unusual in our community, and in my young and sanctimonious mind, I thought it would have been better if they were religious.

My parents sent my two brothers and me to Sunday school when we were young because they wanted us to know other neighborhood kids and be included in the majority community. Once they got older, my brothers stopped attending, but I had a different experience. I enjoyed the teachings and the association with the other members. I have always been a rule-follower, and at church, there were many ways to earn praise and accolades (from leaders and from myself) for participating in the prescribed activities.

I went to church faithfully throughout my teenage years, sitting with a good friend and her family in my congregation. I read the scriptures and prayed daily, and I began to feel a connection with heaven and with God. I attended weekly youth nights throughout the year, plus sleep-away camps in the summer, with fun bonding activities and inspiring, faith-building speakers. I had several experiences in those years that confirmed to me that I was in the right place and doing the right thing.

One concept the leaders taught and reiterated to the youth was the value of marrying someone in the church. They reinforced that this was of utmost importance, and this became my goal. I was not interested in dating anyone who was not of my religion. I wanted to marry someone who had the same beliefs and values I had (including chastity before marriage). I wanted to raise my children in this church and be like the other families I observed who came to church together. I wanted to teach my children about the gospel through the behavior I modeled and the lessons we taught in our home. I wanted to gather my children around me on Sundays to attend church and throughout the week to read from the scriptures. This sounded like a wonderful approach to raising a family, and this is what I strived for.

Bryan and I talked about this a lot throughout our friendship and courtship. We both wanted a family in the church, and we were both willing to do what it took to accomplish that. Unfortunately, that summer when I got back from my freshman year of college, this meant breaking up for a time. One of Bryan's goals was to go on a mission for our church, and we both knew that at the rate we were going, he would not be able to keep the standards long enough to get out on that mission.

Our contention and fighting were almost a cover, a way to make it so we had to break up, because we knew we must. It was still a painful, wretched separation. We both felt dejected and full of gloom the whole summer. I thought about him constantly. I dated other guys during the next few years, but no one compared to him.

Bryan completed one year of college and then went on his mission. He served in New York City for two years. He was an excellent missionary; he worked exceedingly hard, taught many people the gospel, made a lot of friends, and assisted in administrative capacities. Six months into his mission we began writing letters. We were back to a long-distance relationship, and we were back to falling in love. By the time he got home, we knew we wanted to pursue our relationship again. Four weeks later, we got engaged, and within three months, we were married.

Bryan and I did create the family we envisioned. We took our kids to church every Sunday, even on vacation; we read scriptures and prayed individually and as a family and held weekly formal family meetings with gospel teaching; we held positions of responsibility in our congregations that required many hours of our time and no small amount of emotional energy. We did this throughout Bryan's undergraduate education, medical schooling, residency, and years of a busy medical practice. We continued our habit of talking for hours on end, grateful that we didn't have to write long letters anymore to communicate. We felt amazingly fortunate that we got along so well, enjoyed each other's company, and supported each other fully.

I stayed home to raise our four children and take care of the household management. Even though I had excelled in school and enjoyed learning, being a stay-at-home mom was my ultimate dream. I loved taking care of our kids and strived to be the best mom that I could be. I continued to read and learn new things. I often analyzed what I was reading (mostly nonfiction) by taking notes, and I tried to absorb and assimilate the knowledge in my mind. I felt at times that I was not intellectually stimulated or that it would be nice to have a career where I felt competent and important, but I was willing to make this sacrifice to be at home with my kids. I thought that was the best way to raise a family. And it did make life convenient for us. Bryan was able to focus on his studies and then his burgeoning practice, while I took care of household organization. I enjoyed keeping track of the bills and insurance, acquiring and preparing the food, and arranging the kids' playdates and sports or dance classes. Because of my hard work, when Bryan had time off, we were able to play together. We went on dates almost every weekend and went on family outings when he had Saturdays off.

We did not do any leisure activities on Sundays, however. We followed our church's mandate to keep the Sabbath day holy. Sundays were for church attendance (Bryan even came to church after thirty-hour shifts at the hospital), scripture study, church service, and quiet family activities.

I loved the challenges of motherhood. In the beginning, I struggled to learn how to be patient with a toddler's tantrums or how to help my kids be kind to each other. But I worked hard to stay calm and continually practiced new skills and methods of parenting. When I improved in these realms, it was immensely rewarding. I enjoyed reading to my kids, taking them to children's museums, aquariums, and other educationally enriching areas, and doing crafts with them. These efforts paid off when they started school and tested into gifted programs. They were diligent and obedient students. It was fun to watch them learn as they went through school.

I also adored watching them learn about the gospel. They went to Sunday school and participated in the other youth programs I had attended. Bryan and I taught them at home as well. Throughout my teen years, I had many exciting insights and personal inspirations, and I couldn't wait to share these with my kids.

We had high expectations for our kids in keeping with the church standards. We did not allow them to wear tank tops, crop tops, two-piece swimsuits, or short shorts. They couldn't have more than one piercing in each ear or tattoos or piercings anywhere else. They couldn't date until they were sixteen and had restrictions after that about when and how often they could see boys they were interested in. The list of rules and restraints for the youth in our church is long and specific, and we absolutely believed we were doing the right thing by enforcing them. It may sound extreme, but everyone in our community agreed this was the best manner to raise righteous youth. We believed we were setting them up for the life they would want, which, in our minds, was the same as the life we envisioned for them.

I wanted their childhoods to be perfect: in their learning and academic career, in their friends and social activities, and, most importantly, in staying true to the gospel and being united as a family at church.

Then our kids became teenagers. They didn't want to go to the youth activities. This created some conflict, but I understood that it was normal for teenagers to dislike church. The fact that I went of my own volition as a teen was rare.

I worried, however, that they didn't seem to understand and love the church the way I did. Their youth speakers and teachers didn't seem as dynamic and inspiring. Their friend groups weren't as vivacious and supportive of gospel living as Bryan's and mine had been. In short, they were not having the teenage experience that we had.

Bryan and I fretted over this dilemma often. We held liberal political beliefs, especially compared to other church members we knew, and we worried that this had contributed to our kids' tepid feelings about the church. We wondered if we had made the right choice of where to raise our kids, even down to what neighborhood we lived in. We thought if they'd had different friends or different leaders, they would have felt as we did when we were that age. We weren't sure what we did to have such great friend groups in high school and such a vibrant church community as we grew up, so we didn't know how to recreate that for our kids. We felt that our kids' lives were not going how they were supposed to.

Moreover, as some of our kids experienced anxiety and depression in their high school years, Bryan and I added this to our mounting pile of evidence that things were going wrong for our kids and our family. Kaitlin, the oldest, was the first to need counseling and then medication. She had researched antidepressant medicines on the internet and asked us if she could take them. She even knew the acronym SSRI and what it stood for: selective serotonin reuptake inhibitor. Bryan and I questioned this course of action for several reasons. We didn't know how the medications affected someone her age; we didn't trust the pharmaceutical companies and were concerned about the number of people in the nation on these pills;

and most of all, we were uneasy about the stigma. We worried that if other people found out (including Kaitlin's future roommates at college), they would think badly of her (and, more honestly, think badly of us as parents).

Kaitlin was not only the first of our kids to find relief from anxiety and depression through medication and therapy, but she was also the first to have some hesitations about the church. Social media and the internet exposed her to questions and doubts about church doctrine and practices, specifically the inequality of women in the church. This bothered her. She stuck with the church through her college years, but I could tell it wouldn't be forever. It was clear that she was staying in because we wanted her to. We were a close family, and we were still supporting her financially. She was biding her time until she was independent enough to find her own path as far as religion. She often brought up her concerns at Sunday family dinners, to Bryan's and my dismay. We wanted her to be open about her thoughts and questions, but we worried that her doubts would make it more difficult for her younger sisters to believe in the church.

I was more uncomfortable than Bryan when Kaitlin made jokes and shared memes about things that happened in the church. When a high-ranking church leader spoke about how wonderful women are, she said that this was condescending considering the prohibition against women having priesthood authority. She pointed out the thoughtless things leaders said about the LGBTQ community or the church's past racist policies. She made fun of the silly habits of proselytizing missionaries and even made jokes like, "How many church members does it take to change a light bulb?" Answer: "Three. One to say the opening prayer, one to give a spiritual thought, and one to bring the refreshments."

When she said these things, I had flashbacks of my own family growing up. They were not overtly negative about the church or my participation in it, but I knew that they thought it was silly and foolish. My parents and two brothers made snide comments throughout the years that indicated they thought I was naïve and blinded to be so faithful. They brought up things about Christianity and conservatism in general and about my denomination specifically. This voice of derision had been in the back of my head all my life. It varied in intensity throughout the years, but when my kids started to have doubts about the church and mocked some of the teachings, the voice grew louder and harder to ignore.

I told Kaitlin that I was sensitive to church criticism because of this. I explained that she grew up with a family who were supportive of church involvement, and I asked her to imagine what it was like to be the brunt of those kinds of jokes. She tried to joke less about it after that.

When they stopped holding in-person church in March 2020 because of the pandemic, Bryan and I would ride our bikes up the canyon on Sunday mornings. We had long talks on these rides about church and our waning commitment to some of the beliefs. We had been married more than twenty years and had two kids in college. It was a good time to reassess what we wanted in life. We talked about how at this age and stage you see that life is hard and complicated, and the church maybe doesn't have answers to all of life's questions or problems.

Living in the church meant believing that there is one right way to live. According to the church, the path to happiness is only found by stringent obedience to a laundry list of rules and standards, including daily personal and family prayers and scripture reading, weekly family meetings to teach the gospel, regular visits to ailing neighbors, attending weekly church services and keeping the Sabbath day holy, going to periodic congregational activities to meet and strengthen other members, talking to anyone who wasn't a member about the church and encouraging them to join, paying tithing and other donations, fasting once a month, helping the congregation in some assigned role, dressing modestly, and living a strict dietary code.

The route to heaven was precisely delineated and was the same for every person. You must get baptized as a child, get married to someone of your faith, and make efforts to keep everyone in your life active in the church. Men receive the priesthood as teenagers and have corresponding special duties. They are encouraged to be the sole providers for the family, and women are admonished to stay home and raise the children. The overall goal is to live worthily to have the Spirit of Christ always guiding you. If you did that, you could make the best decisions, be forgiven of your sins, and have comfort and guidance throughout your life.

Bryan and I weren't sure that adhering to these teachings was the only or best approach to life anymore. We became disillusioned when we saw people outside the church conducting their lives differently and still experiencing happiness and success.

We realized over the next few months that we didn't miss going to church. Some families in our communities were holding pseudo-church services in their homes, but Bryan and I agreed that we didn't want to do this. We were okay without church teachings or practices for ourselves or our kids for a while.

On one of our bike rides, we stopped at a shady campground along the trail. We sat for a minute at a picnic table, looking around at the clumps of trees interspersed with camping sites. The trees had a hazy green look from the leaves starting to unfurl. The sun shone in the blue sky, and other bikers and pedestrians passed by. We talked about the church again, and I told Bryan that I had stopped reading my scriptures about three months ago. I had grown bored with reading the same thing day after day, year after year. When I first studied church doctrines as a youth, I loved them. There was so much to read and learn and understand. I was fascinated with the concepts and how they could be applied in real life. But over time, those inspirational moments became fewer and fewer. We studied the same scriptural accounts over and over, and every year I got less and less out of them. So, finally, I decided to take a break from scriptures altogether.

Bryan fingered some dried leaves on the picnic table as we talked. We both still wore our bike helmets because we hadn't planned on stopping for this long. He told me he was not bothered by this admission. I figured he wouldn't be. He is tolerant and easy-going in his judgments of others. He explained that he had developed a concept he called "floating." He said, "Sometimes you are paddling or rowing hard down the river, doing all the things you're supposed to and working diligently to make great progress, and sometimes you are floating. You're still in the river, but you're not working as hard. You can take a break from reading scriptures or holding positions of responsibility. It's okay to coast for a while."

I appreciated that he was supportive and had such a forgiving and accepting perspective. However, I did not totally agree with him. I have an all-or-nothing personality. And I believed that the doctrine of our church taught that you do it all or you don't receive salvation. There's no chance *floating* will earn you that highest eternal reward. You must be doing all the things all the time. In addition, I liked being the one who could do all those things. I often reflected that some members had more of an emotional belief in the church but struggled with the required behaviors and standards. My religious faith was less emotional; it was centered on total obedience to the duties and responsibilities of the church, including leading specific classes or groups, assisting with congregational activities, visiting sick or lonely members, and having church lessons and conversations at home with my kids. I was good at doing those tasks, and I liked feeling confident in my abilities. If I stopped doing those things, I feared my beliefs would start to unravel.

Bryan and I discussed this for a few more minutes, and then got back on our bikes and continued our ride. My mind went over the conversation, and I pondered some of the other reasons I was feeling a separation from the church.

Not only was I growing tired of going to church and studying the same scriptures year after year, but I also began to see that, as our kids were growing up, our family may not look like we had visualized. In an ideal world, Bryan and I pictured our kids married to members of our faith, living close to us, and having two to five children. We wanted to have them over for Sunday dinners and babysit the grandkids on weekends while the parents had a date night. We imagined teaching our grandkids about the church, holding some of the same lessons and activities that we'd held with our kids. We wanted everyone to be active and faithful in the church, no dissent or variance.

If it wasn't going to look like this, I wasn't sure I wanted to be a part of it. I didn't want to be the silly and naïve one again, the one who continued being faithful and pious while the others snickered behind my back. I realized my commitment to the gospel standards had as much to do with appearing a certain way, fitting in, and being accepted and praised as it did with believing in the doctrine and the salvation the church offered. There were prominent families in our community who had it all: beautiful, well-behaved children; affluence that afforded them large homes and nice boats; positions of authority and leadership in the church organizational structure. These were the families we aspired to be. These were the lives we hoped to live one day. But a creeping suspicion began to sink in. Logic told me that the percentage of families who end up like this was small. Focusing on them blinded me (and others) to the large number of families who were not living up to that standard and who were, in fact, suffering under the weight of it. This dynamic reminded me of the claims of multilevel marketing companies: "Sell our product and make over $100,000 every month!" When regulatory agencies investigate these assertions, they find that less than one percent of salespeople make anywhere near that amount. The fact that anyone can lures you in though, and makes you believe that you can too. This was the promise of living a righteous life. Your kids will be successful in their education and career, marry a member of our faith and have many children, and stay close to the gospel and to you throughout their lives. When you opened your eyes though, you saw how few families attained that. It was a false promise.

Another layer of my disillusionment started about five years earlier when I was asked to be the president of the women's group of our congregation. This is a three-year position that holds prestige and requires a lot of time and hard work. The president oversees Sunday meetings of the women's group, including music, teachers, and announcements. She coordinates with the other groups (men's, youth, children) in planning and executing congregational activities and taking care of the service and welfare needs of members. She organizes the women into groups who would look out for each other and meet periodically. She visits women in their homes, especially those who were struggling or had stopped coming to church.

I was excited and honored to be invited to fulfill this role. I knew I would enjoy the administrative aspects. I liked getting to know the women, particularly women who moved in during the years I was president. Being assigned to reach out to new people made it easier to do, and the resulting friendships were rewarding. The timing was good too. Sydney, my youngest child, had started kindergarten, and I had some extra time on my hands.

The part that was challenging for me, however, was encouraging women who were no longer coming to church to come back. Another distasteful duty was trying to find interested nonmembers and bring them to church, hoping they would join. I recoiled at both expectations. It felt awkward and unpleasant. I cringed remembering my parents' feelings when their neighbors made similar attempts with them. I felt unscrupulous, and I thought, "If these people don't want to come to church, they shouldn't have to." I was happy to welcome anyone who wanted to come, but I did not want to persuade someone to come who didn't want to.

There was an added layer to this difficulty: I criticized myself because I thought I *should* want to bring people back to church. Why did I not want to? There was clearly something wrong with me and with my values. I should strongly believe that every person in the world would be better off if he or she came to our church and committed to it. Where was my conviction? My faith? If I believed this was *the* true church, the only road to eternal salvation, wouldn't I want everyone to be here with me? These questions bothered me, but I couldn't change how I felt.

I lacked assurance that all people had to be faithful Christians partly because my parents and brothers did not go to church. When your family members don't participate, it is painful to believe that only devout members will go to heaven. I love my family, and I can see that they are kind, wonderful people who have fruitful careers and positive relationships. Some part of me wants to believe that it will be okay for them in the afterlife. Many people in our church don't have nonmembers in their close family to worry about. It's easier for them to believe they are behaving in a manner that qualifies them for paradise after death because everyone around them believes the same thing and is happy and thriving. With so many of my and Bryan's family not in the church, we had a harder time holding on to the certainty that this was the solitary way to salvation.

Added to this was a growing sense of how wide the world is, how many different beliefs and perspectives there are, and how they each think they are correct and best. It was getting harder and harder to be part of a church and a culture where you are pushed to believe and assert that each person must accept this doctrine or be prohibited from God's presence for eternity. I worked around this mentally by deciding that this church was right for me and Bryan and our kids, but not necessarily for everyone.

Our bike ride didn't end at a high ledge with a view of the valley, but philosophically, I felt like I was on a journey up a mountain path, and the view kept getting wider and more expansive. I saw things differently than I did five or ten years ago, and that meant I might make different decisions now about the best course for my life and my family.

CHAPTER 3

Navigating through the Fog

Our first meeting with Dr. Chen, a pediatrician at the TriStar clinic, was in person, but Dr. Chen, Brooke, and I wore masks. Our area was slow to adopt a mask mandate, and when they finally did, it was county by county and city by city. In early September 2020, with the number of Covid cases continuing to increase and with winter approaching, our city government decided to require everyone to wear masks and businesses to put up signs indicating that masks must be worn.

Brooke's therapist, Sarah, had recommended TriStar. When we got back from Lake Powell, Brooke met with the three different therapists I had booked. She didn't have a deep connection with any of them, in part because they held sessions over Zoom, but she deemed Sarah the best fit. After Brooke's initial appointment, I spoke with Sarah for a few minutes. She recommended we find a doctor and get a prescription for antidepressants. Sarah said she liked TriStar because the doctors there offered a genetic test that showed which medications would work best for the patient. This would theoretically save time because often patients had to try two or more types of SSRIs before finding the one that worked best for them. Bryan had experience with this genetic test. Sometimes his patients had it done, and the results helped Bryan decide which pain medicine would be most effective.

The specific doctor Sarah suggested had a long waiting list, but Dr. Chen had openings right away. The TriStar building was about ten minutes from our house in a nondescript office park. The day was hot for September, and Brooke seemed a little apprehensive. I was relieved we were taking this step because I knew it would bring us closer to Brooke finding relief. We didn't wait long in the waiting room before being called back to Dr. Chen's office.

I was not particularly impressed with Dr. Chen. She was petite with long brown hair and seemed a little scattered. Her office was spacious but had a strange layout. We sat on a long couch against one wall. Directly across from the couch was her desk, but it faced the opposite wall. When she typed information into her computer (as she did often), all we could see was her back.

Dr. Chen asked Brooke briefly about the timing and severity of her symptoms. In her quiet voice, Dr. Chen explained the genetic test in detail. She said the results aren't definitive, but they give an idea of which medications will be helpful and whether the specific patient needs more or less than the usual dosage. She took a swab of Brooke's mouth and told us the results would be back in two weeks. I was disappointed that it would take that long, but I reassured myself that Brooke was meeting with her therapist and there was no rush to get on medication.

Throughout the previous summer months, Brooke had been begging to dye her sandy-blonde hair pink. She brought it up again and again, and each time we said no. Bryan and I did not think it was appropriate for a teenager to have dyed hair, and we worried about what it meant that Brooke wanted that and what other people would think if we let her. A teenager with dyed hair did not fit the image we had worked hard to create. We didn't see this as an overly rigid rule; other families in our religious community had similar standards for their children. If Bryan or I saw another teen with colored hair, we would judge them on some level for not fitting in with community norms as well as our kids did.

We didn't like saying no to our kids however, both because we want them to think and act for themselves and because we didn't like them to be angry with us. It was especially hard to say no to Brooke. She had such an endearing, funny way of asking. She'd have a little smile and say, "What if I...did the laundry all summer for you, then would you let me?" or "What if I... promise to get straight A's next year, then can I dye my hair?" She tried to convince us how cute and fun it would be, but we were not swayed. She seemed disappointed when we said no, but she took it well and didn't brood or sulk. Every few weeks, she would ask again.

In mid-August, right about the time Brooke started her junior year of high school, Haley and her friends planned a road trip to Seattle. Brooke wanted to go with them. She wanted to see the Pacific Northwest, and she thought it sounded fun to hang out with the college girls. I was concerned about Brooke missing the first day or two of school. Haley and her two friends wanted Brooke to go, though, and one friend had dropped out, so they needed and wanted a fourth person. We decided to let Brooke go with them.

The trip was a great success. They had fun driving and eating gas station snacks. To save money, they stayed with a family friend of Amanda's in the Seattle area. The family directed them toward the best attractions, including some amazing hikes. The four of them came back in love with the beauty of the area, and they liked the liberal culture too. They enjoyed hanging out together and getting to know each other better. Of course, they got little sleep, but most of them made up for it on the long drive home.

It took me two days after they got home to notice Brooke's earrings. I actually *didn't* notice them. Kaitlin brought it up in a text conversation. She asked what I thought of Brooke's new piercings. I had to go find Brooke immediately; I was flabbergasted that I could have missed such a crucial detail. Sure enough, in addition to her single piercings, Brooke had two new piercings on both lobes, making three in a row on each side. She seemed happy about them and loved the way they looked. I grilled Brooke about when she got them and where. She said Amanda had pierced them while they were on their trip. "Where was Haley?!" I asked. Brooke replied, "She was with us. She encouraged me to do it."

There were many aspects of this that made me angry and frustrated: that it was an at-home piercing instead of a professional one (more likelihood of infection and too spontaneous); that Brooke would want these extra piercings and get them when she knew we didn't approve; and, most of all, that Haley would allow this to happen and even encouraged it. I had trusted Haley to take her little sister on a fun college roadtrip, and she had betrayed that trust. How could Haley think I would be okay with this? Neither of them had thought to ask me or wonder what I thought? In my mind, they knew it was wrong and that I would disapprove, and they were trying to pull one over on me.

"I want you to take them out right now," I told Brooke. I was agitated but not overly angry.

"Why? What's the big deal?" she protested.

I responded, "You know that we only want you to have one piercing in each ear. You knew that and you willfully disobeyed."

She insisted that she didn't think I would care. "Kaitlin has a second earring."

"Kaitlin got hers as an adult. You are still a child, and you still live under our rules. We can maybe discuss more piercings in the future, when you're a little older, but for now, take them out. They're going to get infected anyway."

Brooke did not complain anymore after that. She was compliant and dutiful, as usual. The earrings were out by the end of the day. However, when Bryan and I discussed Brooke's depression on the drive home from Lake Powell, we softened our stance. We realized that our rigid rules may be stifling Brooke's self-expression and intensifying her depression. Up to this point, we had convinced ourselves that enforcing these standards was the best way to parent, but now we questioned that. We both agreed that we should allow Brooke to dye her hair.

A few days after we got back from the trip, I pulled Brooke aside. "Dad and I have decided it would be okay if you dyed your hair." Her face lit up immediately.

"However," I continued, "We don't want it to be too extreme. I want it done by a professional, and I will pay for it. I'll reach out to my hairdresser and see if she can do a light pink. Would that be okay?" Brooke knew she had to take this chance while it was on the table, and she readily agreed. Before this, I had never paid for my kids to have their hair colored, a natural or unnatural shade. But times were changing; it was important to realize that each kid has her own unique needs.

The hair appointment took three hours. Brooke's shoulder-length hair is light on top and darker underneath. The hairdresser had to first bleach it so the dye would show up. The result was a beautiful light pink. Brooke and I were both pleased with how it looked.

Brooke's genetic test results were due back the first week of October. A scheduler at TriStar called a little before that to set up an appointment to go over the test and decide on a medication. Unfortunately, Dr. Chen was out of town for a week right around that time. We couldn't set an appointment until October 9th. The day before that appointment, the office notified me that Dr. Chen had contracted Covid. She was working from home and would still be able to meet with us, but it would be over Zoom.

For a college lecture, Zoom works adequately enough. Students can sign on and listen to the professor. It's convenient to watch from home and not have to trudge over to campus. For a social get together, Zoom's usefulness decreases. Yes, you can all be there, but the lags in speech and silenced words make it difficult to get in sync with each other and have fun. An important informational meeting or appointment is one of the worst times to use Zoom. Trying to take in the pertinent information while having difficulties hearing and understanding each word can be exasperating. This is what we had to deal with for our meeting regarding Brooke's antidepressant medication.

At the appointed time, Brooke and I sat next to each other at the kitchen table with the computer in front of us. It was a Friday afternoon, and the large windows showed a clear blue sky with a few scattered clouds. We clicked on the link and were soon connected. Brooke scrolled through her phone absent-mindedly while I did most of the talking.

Dr. Chen greeted us and apologized for the online meeting. She didn't ask how Brooke was doing but went straight into discussing the genetic test results. She had a printout copy in front of her, and she had sent me an electronic copy. She went through the different medications and whether they would work for Brooke. I switched screens back and forth from the Zoom call to the test results, trying to keep up with where Dr. Chen read from and which medication she referred to. Brooke didn't have much to add. There are many SSRIs to choose from. Picking the first one is a gamble. The test results didn't make the choice easier, in my opinion.

There were five or six medications in Brooke's "green zone," which meant the doctor would prescribe the usual dose, and around the same number in the yellow zone, indicating she'd need a slightly higher dose.

I wished I could hear Dr. Chen more clearly and take better notes; I knew Bryan would ask me later why we chose the one we did. But the connection was poor, and the words were unfamiliar. In the end, we went with Cymbalta. Bryan was confused by that choice when we talked about it that evening. He said even though Cymbalta is technically an antidepressant, it is more often prescribed for certain pain conditions than to treat depression. He trusted Brooke's doctor's opinion, though, and we filled the prescription that night. We had a follow-up appointment in two weeks.

One afternoon a few days later, I walked upstairs to talk to Brooke. At that time, our school district held in-person classes two days a week. The rest of the time, the learning was done online. This was a non-school day, and Brooke was in her room taking a nap. As I walked down the hall, my mind unwittingly scanned through alarming what-if scenarios. What if I walked in her room and something had happened to her? What if she had self-injured or taken something? What if she wasn't breathing? I went through whom I would call and what the rest of the day would look like. These frightful thoughts came often in those weeks. I didn't want to contemplate them, but they came easily, and I couldn't dismiss them.

During the first few weeks of an adolescent taking an antidepressant, the risk of suicide attempts increases. Although it was disquieting, I didn't want to be ignorant of this fact; I wanted to keep it in mind as I monitored Brooke's response to the medication. The rate of teen suicide was particularly high in our area, and when you add on the emotional strain of Covid and at-home schooling, suicide is something every parent should be cognizant of.

When I talked to Bryan about these worries, he dismissed them. He said, "It's not that common." I tried to keep this in mind as I approached Brooke's door, but the what-ifs still flashed through my mind. I opened the door and walked in the room. Brooke was asleep on her bed. I watched her for a moment until I was confident that she was breathing and safe.

The large window to the right had the shade pulled up and revealed a view of the majestic mountains to the east. Underneath the window was a long, cushioned bench—a window seat that we had designed especially for Brooke when we built this house. Tall white bookcases stood on both sides of the window seat, filled with Brooke's YA novels, snow globe collection, and other colorful knickknacks. Over the summer, Brooke had decorated her room to fit her style. The wall surrounding the window and above the bookcases was covered with shining silver CDs. Brooke used a whole case of blank CDs, taped them up in meticulous rows and columns, and the effect was iridescent: hundreds of rainbows shimmering on the metal surfaces in the sunlight. Brooke's bed was against the south wall, across the room from where I stood. Above the wainscoting on this wall, she had attached a string of LED lights, one long strip that extended the length of the wall. Brooke had a remote control for these lights that allowed her to toggle between different colors and intensities. Today they were light pink.

On the wall between the bed and the closet doors, Brooke had hung cow-print vinyl wallpaper. Colorful CDs hung from the ceiling on matching ribbons in front of the black-and-white background. The last wall, to my right, had a row of old records toward the top and a darling collage of pictures lower down—some pictures of Brooke and her friends, some of her favorite movies and bands, and some lively-colored ones for aesthetic appeal. I marveled at how different this look was from Brooke's previous, subtler decorations. The cumulative effect was both artsy and angsty.

I let my eyes wander over the pictures in the collage for a while, admiring Brooke's photography skills and decorating style. She stirred in the bed and sat up. "Good morning!" I teased. It was 1:30 in the afternoon, not an unusual time for Brooke to be sleeping until. She had been generally lethargic since school had started, even though she was only getting up early twice a week. When she went down to the basement to do homework, often I'd find her asleep an hour later, her computer and notebooks spread out around her.

"How are you feeling?" I asked.

Brooke replied, "I'm fine. I can't believe I slept this long; I need to get going on my homework." I noticed Brooke's chipped nail polish. Around her nails, she had picked the skin in a few places until it bled and scabbed over.

"Well, I guess your body needed the sleep, so I'm glad you got it. What are you doing the rest of today, after your homework?"

"Gwen and I might go to the park." Gwen was Brooke's best friend. They met when they were clarinet players in the marching band. Both were smart and motivated in school, and they had the same sense of humor.

"Oh, that's fun. How is Gwen these days? I haven't seen her for a while."

"She's good," Brooke responded. "She's having trouble with her parents again. Her mom is crazy. She makes up a bunch of rules and gets mad and yells, but then she goes off on a week-long trip by herself, and nothing is enforced. Her dad is kind of hot and cold, too. Did I tell you her sister moved back in? Her brother already lives there, and he has a lot of problems. Gwen likes her sister, but there's a lot going on in that house."

"That's too bad. I hope things get better for her." I secretly wondered if Brooke described me as crazy to her friends. It was interesting to hear this because Brooke and Gwen mostly hung out at Gwen's house. Bryan and I wondered if Brooke was embarrassed about our house or us, but she assured us it was no big deal. We encouraged Brooke to bring her friends home, and we even offered to buy pizza or make cookies to lure them here. But she rarely did.

As Brooke got out of bed and started picking up clothes from the floor she said, "Sam might come to the park, too. He's fun to be with, but sometimes I think he likes being with his guy friends more than me and Gwen, and I do *not* like his friends."

"You guys seem to be hanging out more often though, which I think is great." Brooke and Sam were friends for now, but I thought he was the best. He is tall and broad-shouldered, with long, floppy hair and a huge smile. When he comes over, he is polite and talkative; he seems mature and good-natured. Above all, he is thoughtful and kind to Brooke. Kaitlin and Haley had dated guys in high school who were not as nice to them. Those boys didn't respond to texts or plan any dates and often made the girls feel like they were second class. Brooke and Sam weren't dating yet, but I was relieved that Brooke had found a possible boyfriend who was caring and equally as interested in her as she was in him.

"Let me know when you leave," I said as I left Brooke's room.

I was pleased that Brooke was going to hang out with her friends. Besides taking naps in her room, her usual place was on one of two small gray couches in our living room. The entry, living room, and dining room are one big, open area in our house. We didn't let the kids have their computers in their rooms, so when school went online in March because of Covid, Brooke commandeered a spot on the living room couch and did her schoolwork from there. Even when she wasn't doing homework, she curled up on the couch, looking at her phone. For the most part, I liked her there because I could keep an eye on her, but I wasn't sad that she was going somewhere else for a while today.

My dad lives about an hour away from us, and we get together once or twice a month. One Sunday, he came over for dinner. After he greeted everyone in the kitchen and chatted for a minute, Brooke came downstairs.

"Brooke!" my dad boomed with a big smile. "You're not in your usual place!" I guess he had noticed over the last few months that Brooke was often camped out on the gray couch. She laughed and shook her head like, "That's a good one, Grandpa."

Kaitlin and Ben arrived shortly after that, and we put the final touches on dinner. We took the enchiladas out of the oven and brought out the salsa and sour cream. Cups, napkins, and forks were already on the long dining room table, and the plates were stacked on the bar in the kitchen, ready to be filled. As people dished out food and made their way to the table in the next room, my dad noticed Kaitlin's backpack on the floor.

"What is that rainbow handkerchief you've got on your backpack, Kaitlin?"

"It's for gay pride, don't you know, Grandpa?"

"Yeah, but you're not allowed to have anything like that." My dad loved to joke like this. He thought it was funny to tease us about the rules of our religion. I rarely spoke with him directly about religion or any of our beliefs, so he didn't know the extent of Kaitlin's disaffection with the church.

Kaitlin replied, "I can have whatever I want. I want to be an advocate for gay rights."

My dad finished filling his plate and followed Kaitlin to the dining room. The eight chairs around the table were filled, and the glass covering over the wood surface of the table shone in the sunlight. The food smelled appetizing, and we were hungry and excited to eat. We paused the conversation while Bryan prayed over the meal. As we ate, my dad had more to say about Kaitlin's rainbow accessory and what it stood for.

"I'm glad that gay marriage is legal, and I'm all for their equal rights, but I do not understand trans people. When they ask for rights and protections, my mind wonders, where is it going to end?"

Bryan and I nodded our heads, even though we felt more sympathy and understanding for LGBTQ individuals than my dad did. Bryan added, "Yeah, I get gay people, like, I can understand that, but I don't get transgender people. It's strange that they don't feel like they are the gender they were born as. And nonbinary, that's a whole other confusing issue."

Over the years, Kaitlin had been our intermediary in understanding LGBTQ issues. She kept us up to date on related news in the world and in our religious community. She helped us understand new terms and the various nuances and difficulties that segment of the population faced. A few months ago, she had tried to explain that gender was a construct that society made up.

"Most people feel like they are male or female, but there is an in-between," she had explained. "Many people aren't necessarily one or the other. They identify as gender nonbinary, or gender nonconforming." Bryan and I were not convinced. We both thought, "I'm pretty sure gender is a thing." Ever since then it had been a running joke with Bryan to say "it's not binary" when something either/or came up. For instance, if we were talking about a sports competition, Bryan would say, "It doesn't have to be two teams, it's not binary."

As my dad and Bryan talked about this issue over their enchiladas, I could see Kaitlin and Ben exchanging looks, and I also noticed Brooke shifting in her seat. She finally spoke up. "You may not understand it, but that doesn't mean it's not a thing. I feel strongly that all LGBTQ identities should be treated respectfully and should have protections under the law. It bothers me that you don't seem to agree."

Bryan tried to backtrack, "Oh, I agree that they should. It's hard for me to understand the dynamics of that, though, how that feels or what that looks like."

It was Kaitlin's turn to speak up, "Dad, it's hard for you to understand because you come from a place of great privilege." She ticked them off on her fingers, "You have white privilege, male privilege, hetero privilege, and cis-gender privilege. You have all the privileges!"

My dad asked, "What does cis-gender mean?"

Brooke answered his question, "It's when your perceived or experienced gender is the same as what you were assigned at birth. Cis-gender people need to acknowledge their privilege and imagine what it's like to feel the opposite. Trans people aren't weird or wrong or bad, they just are." She seemed flustered and slightly upset. When she finished talking, she looked down at her plate and picked at her food.

Kaitlin was in her senior year of college, majoring in English. She is intellectual, reads avidly, and has a lot of knowledge about women's issues and the intersectionality of feminist thought and LGBTQ issues. Her honors thesis was almost done; its title was "Seeking the Feminine Divine: Women's Religious Authority, Power, and Presence in Twentieth Century Poetry." She was well prepared to educate us on this topic.

"Many people find it difficult to understand gender nonconformity. Humans love the binary. Our brains naturally tend toward two options and nothing in between. That seems satisfying. But there are many times when the binary does not explain the whole of reality. Sticking to binary systems such as male/female, body/spirit, and reason/emotion cuts you off from the exciting, interesting parts in between. Additionally, we frequently put dualistic differences into a value system, one good and one not as good. For example, the male/female binary gets distorted into superior/inferior. The spirit is seen as holier than the body, which should be overcome. In Western culture, we value reason over emotion. And this plays into the patriarchy because women are associated more with emotion and men with reason, and women have the bodily experience of giving birth while men seem more in tune with their spirit because they don't have babies. Christianity maintains male monotheism, which reinforces the social hierarchy of patriarchal rule: God is above men who are in turn above women. Therefore, a lot of feminists encourage thinking outside the binary, and that resonates with gender nonconforming individuals."

My dad sat back with an impressed but bemused look on his face. He wasn't done pushing buttons. "It sounds like you don't believe that a woman's place is in the home," he said, as he gave a little chuckle. Kaitlin rolled her eyes. He continued, "But seriously, your church doesn't recognize anything more than two genders, right? And they're not exactly advocating for gay rights."

There was an uncomfortable pause and some shifting glances. None of us felt at ease with our church's policies on LGBTQ issues. Some were more bothered and offended than others. Bryan and I had discussed our feelings about it throughout the years. We felt strongly that gay marriage should be legal (even though our church lobbied strongly against that), and that LGBTQ people shouldn't be discriminated against at work or in public settings. We believed that they should have equal opportunities and be allowed to express themselves and be who they are. But when it came to our church's policies and practices, we looked the other way. We knew the church viewed homosexuality as a sin and that they wouldn't let LGBTQ people participate in many of the church ordinances and practices. They can join worship services and lessons, but if they are too loud or ostentatious, they are deemed a "distraction." The rules about what you can and can't do vary from congregation to congregation, but in general the church does not recognize gay marriage as valid or as "ordained of God," and gay or trans individuals are not allowed to serve in leadership positions.

However, we didn't have to face these issues head-on because we didn't have anyone close to us who identified as LGBTQ. We felt that the church was a benefit to us and our family in so many ways that we were willing to overlook these intolerant and prejudiced beliefs. We understood those who didn't feel the same beneficence toward the church, though. We didn't blame gay people or their families for leaving the church.

As my dad looked from Brooke to Kaitlin for an answer, I finally spoke up, "No, they don't. They embrace the binary wholeheartedly. Maybe someday they will accept LGBTQ members more fully. It's a struggle for those individuals right now. I know a lot of members who would like the church to be more open, but the leadership isn't ready yet."

"Because they are all old, white men," Kaitlin added.

It was time to change the subject. "Who's ready for dessert?" I asked.

CHAPTER 4

A Growing Discomfort

In my twenties, I read *Dead Man Walking* by Sister Helen Prejean, a member of the Sisters of St. Joseph congregation of the Roman Catholic Church.[1] This book opened my eyes to the racist nature of capital punishment in America. I learned that not only is the color of the defendant's skin a large determinant in who receives this sentence, but the victim's race also plays an outsized role. A high percentage of death row inmates are Black or some other minority. Most are poor and without the means to retain adequate legal representation, and if the victim was white, the likelihood of capital punishment is much higher than if the victim was Black.

In the book, Sister Prejean writes letters to two condemned death row inmates and becomes their spiritual advisor in the months leading up to their executions. Through this experience, she gains insight into the processes surrounding executions and how those proceedings affect everyone involved: the attorneys, judges, families of the victims, and other inmates. Because of what she saw and learned, she spoke out against capital punishment and advocated for a moratorium on the death penalty.

The book is gripping. Through detailed research and poignant stories, she brings the reader into the U.S. legal and prison systems. She gives an unvarnished presentation of death row and execution conditions. The data she presents clearly shows that capital punishment is not only barbaric in application but also completely ineffectual as a deterrent to violent crime.

The racially discriminatory practices of the criminal justice system shocked me. Before this, I had never given the death penalty much thought. I knew that people in my religious community were for it, but I felt uneasy with that stance. This book crystallized ideas that had been swirling in my head and presented facts and statistics to convince me that a pervasive racial prejudice exists in the application of the death penalty.

After reading this book, it was as if my eyes were open to racial injustices everywhere. Most people would admit racial discrimination in employment. The data clearly shows that Black people make less money than whites for the same work and that Black people have less wealth overall. But there are many other areas of discrimination in America. In the years after I read *Dead Man Walking*, I paid attention when I heard news stories or read magazine articles about other, more subtle, forms of racism, and there were numerous such stories.

I heard about how Black students are disciplined faster, more often, and with more severe consequences than white students. Black rental applicants are denied acceptance. Black people receive smaller mortgage loans with higher interest rates than white people with the same credit history. Black college students are not accepted into sororities and fraternities as often as white students. There was even a news story about the trending hashtag #airbnbwhileblack. The anchor explained that when Black people have their picture on their Airbnb profile, they are denied rentals even if the calendar showed openings. When they changed their profile to a generic photo and a more white-sounding name, they were able to rent.

After learning about these and other difficult situations, I had no doubt that systemic racism was a real and active problem in our society. But many people around me didn't seem to feel the same way. This was confusing and frustrating until I understood some common biases and human tendencies that make it hard for people to recognize and acknowledge unfair circumstances in society.

There is a human inclination to generalize our experience to others. We assume that what happens in our world is similar to what happens in the greater world. It is difficult for us to keep in mind problems that aren't right in front of us. For example, the elementary school my children went to was large but well-run. The building was safe and modern, the teachers and staff were capable and kind, and the curriculum and resources professional and plentiful. Sometimes I find myself thinking about the schools in my area and wondering, what could be wrong with education in America? It seems to me like things are going fine.

However, I have taken the time and effort to become aware of the bigger picture. Because funding for schools is largely based on property taxes, the quality of education in the U.S. can vastly differ based on location. The relative lack of funds in poorer areas results in fewer qualified teachers, larger class sizes, more buildings in disrepair, and fewer opportunities for extracurricular activities. If I didn't push myself to learn about other places, I would continue to believe that most schools are like the ones in my area.

The same thing occurs with employment, college, and housing opportunities. White people like me tend to assume others have the same prospects that we do. We think about a different group of people, maybe a minority group, and wonder how it could be so hard to be successful. We have a sneaking suspicion that maybe they are doing something wrong, or maybe they have an inherent weakness.

The fundamental attribution bias that exists in all of us makes us think that when others make mistakes or don't succeed, it is because of their character or something internal to them. It is difficult for humans to see the outside forces that affect someone else's behavior. We assume their circumstances are perfect and they messed up because they didn't try hard enough. In general, we don't recognize that the structures we function under result in some groups succeeding and other groups struggling. Because we don't see the structure that favors us, we believe the other group needs to work harder to accomplish what we've accomplished. But the truth is, no matter how hard members of minority groups work, the cards are stacked against them, and they will likely never have the same outcome.

Humans also have a bias that the way things are now is the way things are supposed to be. Believing this helps us feel like our world makes sense and nothing has gone wrong. Another blind spot humans suffer from is confirmation bias. If we already believe that there is no racism in America, we listen to information that agrees with that view and disregard stories or news items that do not.

With these biases as part of our nature, it's no wonder people deny the existence of racial problems in America. The first step then is to become aware of our preconceptions and misconceptions. Only then can we dismantle them and open our eyes to what is happening and what our role is in the oppressive system. I find it easier than some to perceive the biases in myself. I am not perfect at it, but I am willing to admit that they are there. I see my natural inclination to believe one way, but the flaws in that thinking are also apparent to me. The inherent injustices of society seem obvious to me, but others have a harder time perceiving them.

One night I saw Ta-Nehisi Coates on *The Colbert Report*.[2] Bryan and I loved Stephen Colbert's parody of a news show and watched it faithfully. I had never heard of Coates before, but he was a captivating guest. He spoke about his recently published article "The Case for Reparations" in the June 2014 issue of *The Atlantic*.[3] The next day, I ordered a copy of the magazine. I was so taken by Coates that I wanted to own the physical copy of the magazine and not just read the article online. I also purchased his book, *Between the World and Me*, and read it right away. I found Coates' writing persuasive, visceral, and powerful. This was another step in my racism-in-America education.

In the "Reparations" article, Coates details the history of Black people in America, from slavery to Jim Crow to the Civil Rights movement and up to today. Even though I had been interested in and read books about the Black experience and racial issues in America for many years, I learned a lot from this article. I learned that because of a lack of post–Civil War education and opportunity, sharecropping was basically legalized slavery. I learned that Black veterans of World War II were not offered GI bills for college at as high of rates as white veterans. I learned of the malicious, government-backed practice of redlining, where red lines on community maps showed realtors and mortgage brokers where Blacks could and could not buy houses. From similar articles, I learned about thriving Black neighborhoods that were decimated when the U.S. government built the extensive system of interstate highways.

These policies and discriminatory practices led to Blacks holding less wealth, living in poorer areas, and receiving less quality education and fewer opportunities for employment. Despite these terrible practices, Black people persevered. They tried to labor within the arrangements they were given. They struggled to work hard and make a better life for their children. But every time they got ahead, in politics or education or housing, society found a way to push them back down. I felt shocked and repulsed as I discovered the extent of discriminatory practices and the coordination of systemic racism that Black people had been living with for centuries. We are taught to believe that if you work hard, you will be rewarded. But Coates' writing helped me see that this was not the reality in America.

Coates wrote his book *Between the World and Me* as a letter to his son describing what it's like to live as a Black man in America. He explains to his son, "I write you in your fifteenth year. I am writing you because this was the year you saw Eric Garner choked to death for selling cigarettes; because you know now that Renisha McBride was shot for seeking help, that John Crawford was shot down for browsing in a department store."[4] In that same year, Tamir Rice was murdered by the police, and Marlene Pinnock, a grandmother, was beaten and left on the side of the road. Coates tells his son, "And you know now, if you did not before, that the police departments of your country have been endowed with the authority to destroy your body."[5] He says it doesn't matter if the destruction results from an overreaction, a misunderstanding, or a foolish policy. If you make a simple mistake, he admonishes his son, your body can be destroyed.

Furthermore, "The destroyers will rarely be held accountable. Mostly they will receive pensions. And destruction is merely the superlative form of a dominion whose prerogatives include friskings, detainings, beatings, and humiliations. All of this is common to Black people. And all of this is old for Black people. No one is held responsible."[6]

Coates says he is afraid for his son, "but I was afraid long before you, and in this I was unoriginal. When I was your age, the only people I knew were Black, and all of them were powerfully, adamantly, dangerously afraid."[7] When he was his son's age and living in Baltimore, he had to stay vigilant to avoid walking certain blocks and at certain times of day to retain "control over my body."[8]

Coates recounts one of his most frightening experiences—being pulled over by the notoriously violent Prince George County police in Washington, D.C. He knew "…these officers had my body, could do with that body whatever they pleased, and should I live to explain what they had done with it, this complaint would mean nothing."[9] A short time later, he picked up *The Washington Post* and saw that an officer from that same police department had killed a Black man. He read the article as he held his then one-month-old son, and he was shocked to discover that the victim was a friend of his from Howard University, Prince Jones.

He talks about how we have attempted to reform the police through diversity and sensitivity training and body cameras, but these efforts

> …understate the task and allow citizens of this country to pretend that there is real distance between their own attitudes and those of the ones appointed to protect them. The truth is that the police reflect America in all of its will and fear, and whatever we might make of this country's criminal justice policy, it cannot be said that it was imposed by a repressive minority. The abuses that have followed from these policies—the sprawling carceral state, the random detention of Black people, the torture of suspects—are the product of democratic will.[10]

A few years later, I was drawn to the writings of James Baldwin. I first read about Baldwin in an essay about his home in France. I was intrigued and decided to make 2020 my "year of Baldwin." I read his fiction and nonfiction and two biographies about him. In his books, I heard many of the same things I'd read in Coates' *Between the World and Me.* This was disheartening, considering Baldwin was born fifty years before Coates. Why were they talking about the same problems? Why had nothing changed?

I had these ideas stewing in my mind when, on May 25, 2020, George Floyd was murdered by a police officer in Minneapolis, Minnesota, in front of scores of people. The world went into an uproar. Why did this keep happening? Why did the police of America have such disregard and apparent contempt for the "Black body," as Coates says? As more and more stories came out about police violence against Black and brown people, I came back to Baldwin's words many times, astonished at their relevance.

In his debate at Cambridge against William F. Buckley, Baldwin explained,

> You have been through a certain kind of mill and the most serious effect is not the catalogue of disaster—the policeman, the taxi driver, the waiters, the landlady, the banks, the insurance companies, the millions of details twenty-four hours of every day which spell out to you that you are a worthless human being. It is not that. By that time, you have begun to see it happening in your daughter, your son or your niece or your nephew. You are thirty by now and nothing you have done has helped you escape the trap. But what is worse is that nothing you have done, and as far as you can tell, nothing you can do, will save your son or your daughter from having the same disaster and from coming to the same end.[11]

Another time he said, "I'm certain that most white Americans I have encountered, I'm sure they have nothing against me, that's really not the question. The question is really a kind of apathy and ignorance, which is the price we pay for segregation. That's what segregation means, you don't know what's happening on the other side of the wall, because you don't want to know."[12]

America isn't officially segregated anymore, but we certainly are unofficially. White people don't know what's happening on the other side of the wall because they are able to live lives where they rarely encounter those people or those situations. They stay unknowing and apathetic because they can.

The Floyd murder was tragic, and I felt heartsick. These were issues I had read about and cared about for years, and now they received more attention than ever. It was discouraging to hear the accounts of police brutality and the statistics of unfair treatment in all realms of the criminal justice system. I read and discussed these issues with Bryan and my kids, but the people in my area and in my church did not feel the same way as I did. Most of them were political conservatives and quick to defend police actions and criticize or blame minority populations for their problems. Whereas I was sympathetic to and supportive of the many groups of protestors that summer, my friends were more likely to characterize them as violent rioters. I found it best to not discuss the subject with my fellow churchgoers.

I started following anti-racist/anti-bias educators on Instagram, and that fall I read *Me and White Supremacy* by Layla Saad.[13] In the book, she explains white privilege, the unearned advantages whites have by virtue of the color of their skin. Examples of these advantages include knowing that wherever you go your culture will be represented, in the majority, and considered "normal." White people are in company with people of their same color most of the time; in addition, they see white people in books, music, children's toys, movies, and TV. White people in America aren't asked for ID when using a credit card for purchases, aren't asked to speak for their whole race, don't need to talk to their children about race, and don't have to worry about worse health outcomes if they go to the doctor or hospital. Most white people take these things for granted, of course, because they do not know that people of color don't have the same benefits. White people don't understand that their hard work has a different outcome than the hard work of their non-white peers.

Learning about another concept, "white saviorism," was an aha moment for me. I immediately knew that I had assumed and participated in this. White saviorism is a belief that people of color need to be helped or saved because they are less advanced than white people. The truth is minorities live under a system of oppression created and propagated by white people. We create an unjust structure, and then we expect gratitude for helping people out of it. When white people start charities without consulting anyone from the group they want to help or go on mission or service trips to Africa, they are participating in white saviorism. We rarely ask people of color what they need or how they think we can help. We have all the answers and condescendingly "share" with them the bounty we accumulated through the inequitable arrangements in America. Nigerian-American writer Teju Cole summed up this concept in a tweet: "The white savior supports brutal policies in the morning, founds charities in the afternoon, and receives awards in the evening."

In the 1965 debate at Cambridge, James Baldwin said, "It is a terrible thing for an entire people to surrender to the notion that one-ninth of its population is beneath them…I am not a ward of America; I am not an object of missionary charity. I am one of the people who built the country."[14]

As I read about these concepts in Saad's book, I felt myself nodding my head. I had not known the terms, but once identified, I concurred with their existence. Saad reminds us that it is important to think of racism not in terms of a racist joke or a single person being discriminated against, but as a system of advantages based on skin color. All the organizations white people participate in to create a better life for themselves have the odds stacked against Black people. These arrangements consistently produce favorable outcomes for white people and unfavorable outcomes for people of color, specifically Black people. The outcome shows the racism—whether you think of yourself as a racist or not, you are participating in racism.

In the fall of 2020, I started listening to the *Code Switch* podcast by NPR. The podcast's website describes *Code Switch* as "the fearless conversations about race that you've been waiting for….We explore how race affects every part of society—from politics and pop culture to history, food, and everything in between." It quickly became one of my favorite podcasts.

One episode had a profound effect on me. I can remember the street I was driving on when I heard it, heading east and looking at the resplendent mountains shining from the rays of the setting sun. One line struck me like a punch to the gut: "White Christian churches have never reformed and have never faced [the racist] assumptions from their past.

White Christian churches are anchor points for white supremacy in our society."[15]

The speaker was Robert P. Jones, the author of *White Too Long: The Legacy of White Supremacy in American Christianity* and the CEO of the Public Religion Research Institute. Jones is a white Southern Baptist who grew up in Mississippi and once considered becoming a pastor. His research institute created the American Values Survey to study people's values and beliefs and how they change over time. Results from the surveys show that white Christians are in fact unique among voters, especially in their views of race and racism in America. This group had a large influence on the election of 2020. They are unusually active in politics and voting. Although they comprise 15% of the general population, they consistently make up 25% of voters.

Jones explained that white Christians have always believed their version of Christianity is God's means of bringing salvation to a lost world. In the past, I have thought of this as important soul-saving work, but now that sentiment sat differently with me. Their "munificence" is patronizing and self-centered, implying that what other people have is not of value and that everyone needs to be a certain way (the white Christian way) to have God's favor. I realized that Christians do not want to listen to or learn from other groups; more likely, they want to change them. This bothered me.

Jones elucidated the history of the Southern Baptist Convention, the largest protestant denomination of any kind and the dominant expression of protestant Christianity in America, and how they became such a strong voting bloc. The SBC was created when it split from northern Baptists over the question of slavery. Most people think that the decisive issue for evangelical Christians is abortion, but the key concern that ignited their political activism was Brown v. Board of Education, when the Supreme Court made segregation of public institutions unconstitutional. After this decision, whites-only Christian schools popped up all around the south. In the early 1970s, the leaders of these schools came together to protect their "segregation academies" from forced integration. Alliances created from these battles became the foundation for the emerging religious right.

In the 1960s, white Christians championed a massive resistance to the civil rights movement and greatly hindered its progress. They have consistently been on the wrong side of these issues, and according to the results of Jones' research, they still have a hard time connecting the dots and seeing the structural social justice issues at stake. Jones' survey asks a wide variety of questions about white supremacy and systemic racism. He found a clear pattern of white evangelicals holding more racist attitudes, such as denying the existence of ingrained racism, supporting the confederate flag, and denying the need for police reform. On a scale of 1-to-10 for racist opinions, white evangelicals scored 8/10. They topped out the list. Other white Christian groups scored 7/10. No other groups were more consistently either unable or unwilling to see institutional racism in the country.

At this point in the podcast, Jones spoke the words that had such an impact on me: "White Christian churches have never reformed and have never faced [the racist] assumptions from their past. White Christian churches are anchor points for white supremacy in our society." To drive this point home, the podcast hosts quoted a statement Jones made to NBC news. Keep in mind that Jones himself is a white evangelical Christian. In the interview, he said, "The heartbreaking truth is that without white evangelicals, the primary issue that has rent the soul of America since our beginnings, the struggle for racial equality and justice, would suddenly become much more manageable."

These words sunk deep within me, and my heart confirmed their truth. I started to see Christianity as a whole and my involvement in it in a new way. Already bored with the doctrine and the lessons, I felt increasingly troubled that I was associated with an organization that had a history based in white supremacy and a leadership who would not or could not acknowledge that fact, apologize for it, and attempt to reconcile it.

I did not belong to the Southern Baptist church, but these dynamics were present in all white Christian churches. The SBC is the largest protestant denomination and therefore influential over other Christian churches. All Christian churches ignore the fact that for the majority of American history, their ministers have spoken with passion and vigor in favor of slavery, segregation, and white supremacy. Without confronting and dealing with this history, Christian churches implicitly condone that past and remain unable to see the present racial problems clearly. This is apparent in their current actions. For example, when stories of police brutality or statistics of racist practices are covered in the media, Christian institutions and leaders fail to speak out directly against racism and white supremacy and instead take refuge in vague calls for prayer and healing.

In the months after hearing that podcast, I reflected on this issue many times. I felt uncomfortable and embarrassed that I didn't see this dynamic before. I comprehended that I was partially responsible for the continued oppression of Black people in America. Later, I came across a quote from liberation theologist William James Jennings: "White supremacy is a parasite and Christianity, its host."

My church sect didn't allow Black males to be in leadership positions or participate in ordinances of salvation until 1978. That change is celebrated and lauded, but there was never any apology or explanation for the centuries of discrimination. My denomination continues to sideline minority populations. To this day, they don't allow females or LGBTQ members to hold leadership positions. They actively opposed gay marriage before it became legal and continued to speak of its evils afterward. We, along with most Christian churches, have a history of excluding and discriminating against marginalized groups.

Besides creating a growing discomfort with the racial past of my church, listening to anti-racist educators over the course of 2020 made me realize I needed to get more comfortable with people who are different from me. This was a new desire for me. Even though I cared deeply about anti-racist issues throughout my adulthood, I also wanted to conform to my community. I have the same insecurities most people have and, in the past, felt that if I reached out to people who didn't look and act like me, I might not be accepted by my mainstream group. To be honest, that sense of community and approval was at times more important to me than the doctrine and teachings of Christ. I tried to be humble in acknowledging this and realized that it would take time to change those habits of thoughts and actions. But I wanted to try.

There are few racially diverse people where I live so I needed to think of a different way to accomplish my goal. I realized that the LGBTQ community might be a good place to start. Here was another marginalized group whom I cared about in theory but had never spent time with. I began learning more about their issues and reading their stories. I was full of enthusiasm for social justice and wanted to reach out to that group to show love and acceptance and somehow help in their fight for equality.

There was a center in my area for LGBTQ youth to hang out, make friends, and receive mental health services, and they needed adult volunteers. I could help there to get out of my comfort zone, hear about their experiences, and find out how to be of use. Because of the pandemic, however, they were closed. I made a mental note to try again when things went back to normal.

CHAPTER 5

Haley

If the members of our family were listed in order of how often they talked when we were together, Kaitlin would be on the top of that list. On a pie chart graphing percentage of talk time, her slice would be large. She knows a lot about many different subjects and can convey her thoughts well. She also has opinions on a lot of political and social topics. I love talking with her because she easily keeps the conversation going, and I always learn something from her.

Bryan would be the next most frequent speaker. He is animated, talkative, and witty. This is one of the things I love most about him: he makes any party fun and always keeps the crowd laughing. People want him around because he is so entertaining. When we're alone, he continues to be amusing; sometimes he gets me laughing until tears come to my eyes.

Sydney does not talk much when our family is together, mostly because she's the youngest and knows the least about the topics we discuss. After Sunday dinners, she often goes over to the gray couches and looks at her phone while we continue talking. I worry that she feels left out or not important, and I try to bring her into the conversation whenever I can by asking her questions or steering the conversation toward topics that I know she's interested in.

Haley would be tied with Sydney for the bottom of the list. Haley has been less talkative ever since she was a child. Maybe this was a result of Kaitlin's continuous talking, or maybe it's just Haley's personality. As a toddler, Kaitlin had so much to say that we had to limit her to telling us three things before we closed the door for bedtime. Haley didn't need to talk because Kaitlin always did. Haley played easily by herself; she didn't fuss or ask for much.

She continued to be reserved throughout her teen years. We were concerned that she might struggle in her future relationships and that she wasn't communicating important things to us. Sometimes it seemed the only reason she talked to me was to ask me to buy her hair or skincare products, new clothes, or jewelry. We made a rule at one point that before I would buy something for her, she had to tell me three things about her life.

Despite being quiet at home, Haley made friends easily at school. She has a darling personality that is full of humor and charm. She loves spending time with friends. She's a thoughtful listener and a great gift-giver. She made many friends her freshman year of college, but she admitted that she relied a lot on Amanda to be the outgoing one. After her freshman year, in the summer of 2020, Haley decided to take two years off from college and go on a mission to share the gospel full-time. Our church has a formal proselytizing program. They assign young adults a location to serve in and provide training, a furnished apartment, and a companion to be with.

Haley put a lot of thought and prayer into this decision. She had always been a religious person. During her teen years, we often found her on the floor in her bedroom, reading her scriptures and taking notes in a journal. She graduated from the same four-year early-morning religion class that Kaitlin took (the early hours weren't as hard on her as they were on Kaitlin, but it was still a sacrifice). She felt it was her duty and her honor to spread the good news of the gospel to those who did not have the benefit of that knowledge. She believed that the church had blessed her life deeply, and she wanted to offer those blessings to others.

I had reservations about Haley serving a mission. I was becoming disillusioned with the church and started thinking that I might not stay long term. I worried that my zeal and fervor about the church in past years had influenced her decision (of course it had) and that she would feel betrayed when I decided not to participate in church anymore. On the other hand, I wanted to be supportive of her feelings and her choice. It would be confusing and harmful if I spoke negatively about the church at this point. I felt conflicted. I wanted to be open with my kids, but I wasn't sure what I was going to do. I knew that sometimes people go through phases of waning interest in the church but eventually come out of it and are more committed than ever. I didn't feel like that was going to happen to me, but I didn't want to take the chance of ruining my kids' views of the church in case it did.

When Haley first talked about going on a mission, Covid had just started. Like many other shocking and unprecedented events of that time, the church had all the missionaries outside the U.S. sent home within a matter of days. The missionaries could choose to be done with their missions at that time or be reassigned somewhere in America. In the U.S., the missionaries stayed in their apartments, making calls and teaching lessons from their cell phones. For some missionaries this was productive. They loved being able to still teach with the use of technology. For many, however, staying inside with one other person they barely knew and looking at a phone screen all day was a recipe for anxiety and depression.

Haley decided to apply, despite the restrictions of Covid, and we naïvely hoped that the world would be back to normal by the time she left. She applied in May, got her assignment in June (which she read to us and others over Zoom from Amanda's house in Atlanta), and was scheduled to leave at the end of October.

Part of the application process was a mental health review. After Haley filled out the initial paperwork, the church requested that she talk with a counselor to determine if she was emotionally and mentally ready for the intense work of a mission. Haley had dealt with some depression and anxiety in high school and in her freshman year of college. She had seen a therapist briefly two different times, but she had never been on medication. She was open and honest about her struggles, and she felt like she would be able to succeed on her mission. That is the hard part about mental health: no one knows whether it's going to get worse or better or what situations will activate more difficulties. Working hard on an intense challenge like a mission could bring out the best in someone and give her confidence and gusto, or it could make her emotional problems worsen. It didn't seem right to let that fact stop a person from trying, though.

Haley passed the counselor's review and was assigned to Albuquerque, New Mexico. After a three-week preparation course, she would serve there for eighteen months. Some missionaries were still getting called to go to places outside of the U.S., but they were sent somewhere in America until the specific foreign country was open and safe. We were glad that Haley would go to a city in America, and we didn't have to worry about where or when a reassignment might take place.

The first week of October, Haley started her mission training program. Usually, the missionaries came together for their preparation instruction, but because of Covid, the church had the missionaries stay home during these weeks. I cleared out the office, and Haley set up her computer and notebooks on the desk for her three-week training period. She woke at 6:30 every morning, listened to Zoom classes during the day, and studied on her own in the evenings. The behavioral expectations during this time included getting up and going to bed at certain times, reading or listening only to spiritual books or music, and having no contact with boys. Haley diligently followed every rule. She took notes during class and reviewed them afterward, filled her Google drive with uplifting music, and role-played different teaching scenarios to improve her capabilities. She memorized scriptures and lessons until she was fluent with both. She enjoyed this time of training and was excited to get to New Mexico to put her skills into practice.

In the middle of Haley's three-week preparation period, Brooke and Sydney had a few days off from school for fall break. We rented a condo in a city three hours south of where we lived. The warm weather, beautiful red rock scenery, and hiking opportunities there made it one of our favorite "local" places to vacation. Bryan's brother Mike, his wife, Josie, and their four children joined us. The condo was big enough for all of us to comfortably sleep and had a large kitchen and living room area. This meant we could eat most meals there, which was cheaper and more convenient than eating out every meal. Kaitlin and Ben came with us, as well as Haley. She had a room to herself and continued her Zoom meetings and studying. When she didn't have class, she joined us for meals and hikes. The rest of us swam in the pool, played board games, and hung out together.

Mike and Josie have three boys and a girl, similar ages as our kids. We hadn't spent a lot of time together when the kids were little because we lived on opposite sides of the country. We only saw them about once a year. But in the last year, they had moved to our city and built a house on our street. We were thrilled to have them closer. Mike and Bryan are good friends, and our two families have a lot in common. They were the only other family on Bryan's or my side who had stable marriages and jobs and were as religious and committed to the church as we were. In addition to that, we got along splendidly and laughed a lot when we were together.

One evening, we went on a hike. The sun was low in the western sky and the air temperature had cooled off to a comfortable seventy degrees. As we walked over the sandy patches in between the rocky terrain, Bryan said to me, "Did I tell you that President Wainwright wants to meet with me?" President Wainwright was the church leader over the regional area. We call the leaders of a congregation bishops, and President Wainwright managed six congregations (and their bishops) in a unit we called a "stake." At the mention of President Wainwright, Kaitlin and Haley perked up and listened more intently.

I said, "No, you didn't." The pathway was not steep, but the sandy areas were expanding, and I had trouble steadying my steps. Cool pockets of air passed by us as we got deeper into the canyon. The walls of the red rock cliffs were wavy, and the horizontal lines etched on them added to the feeling of motion.

Bryan went on, "I am sure he will ask me to be president of the men's group *again*." He seemed slightly irritated, which surprised me. Usually, Bryan relished assisting in the church. He continued, "I've already done that three times, and he knows that." He tried to make a joke of it, "They must be desperate if they're asking me again."

Because the leadership of our church is unpaid, it is customary to rotate the responsibilities to avoid burdening any one person. The president of the men's group was a time-consuming role. It was like what I had done for the women's group, but I was a stay-at-home mom, so the work fit easily into my day. Bryan had a full-time job, and he sometimes questioned the extra work the church asked of him (and all of us) during his time off.

About a month before, I had been asked to be a counselor to the president of the women's group. This job wasn't as difficult as being president, but it was still a prominent position in the church and required no small amount of work. Bryan and I found it ironic that the leaders kept asking us to fulfill these roles when, inside, we were pulling away from the church. We facetiously thought maybe they knew that and were trying to keep us tethered. We didn't say those things to anyone else, though.

Bryan continued with his humor, "I guess I didn't do a good enough job the first three times; maybe I will get it right this time." He also added, "The current president is laid back, so at least there won't be high expectations."

The kids were intrigued that Bryan would say anything negative about church duties. They scrambled over the uneven rocks to get closer to him. We had taught them that serving in the church was an honor and a blessing and that much was expected from whom much had been given. I knew Bryan wanted to be a good example to them and have a positive attitude. But he was clearly displeased with this possibility.

I said, "We'll have to see what he says. When is the meeting?"

"Monday night after we get back. I'm going to tell him I'm only doing the bare minimum. And if there are people who don't want to come to church, I'll be like, that's fine, let them be."

Kaitlin and Haley glanced at each other with surprise and humor in their eyes. They knew, as I did, that Bryan wouldn't say that. We knew that he would accept the assignment and work hard to be a great president. That was the only way Bryan knew how to do things. He was highly capable, efficient, organized, and hardworking. He succeeded in everything he did, and he enjoyed the praise from church leaders for doing a good job.

The Friday after we got back from our fall break trip, Brooke and I went in for a follow-up appointment with Dr. Chen. Brooke had been on Cymbalta for two weeks. Even though Brooke was sixteen and could have gone to the appointment alone, I wanted to be there to hear what the doctor thought and to know what instructions were given. When we got called back to the office, Dr. Chen had us sit on the couch against the wall. She got out her stethoscope and listened to Brooke's heart and then took her blood pressure. As she put the equipment away, she seemed flustered and awkward. She spoke quietly but continuously about the effectiveness of Cymbalta and how long it takes until most patients feel better. I couldn't quite catch all of it; she was speaking into the cabinet where the equipment was stored, and then toward her computer on her large white desk. She asked Brooke vague questions about how she was doing and if she thought the medication was working.

Brooke said, "I feel about the same, maybe a little better." I knew that Brooke might be adding in that last part to be agreeable. The doctor typed some information into the computer and then half turned toward Brooke, keeping her fingers on the computer keyboard.

"Any suicidal thoughts?" she asked casually.

"No, not really," Brooke responded. Dr. Chen did not look Brooke in the eyes; she did not elaborate on what she meant by suicidal thoughts. She didn't ask about intensity of thoughts, access to suicide methods, or intent or desire to self-harm in other ways. She asked one yes-or-no question and then typed more into her computer. It seemed like she hoped the answer would be no, so she could move on with her day.

"Okay, let's keep going with this medication. I'll give you a prescription for thirty days this time. Make an appointment on your way out for a month from now. Thanks!"

That was it, short and sweet. With some effort, we got up off the squishy, low couch and walked out. This appointment was mostly to assess any negative side effects that might have shown up right away. Antidepressant medications can take six weeks or more until they elevate the patient's mood. Brooke would stay on this one and see if it worked. If she didn't feel significant effects in a month, we would switch to another type of SSRI. There was nothing to do but wait.

On the drive home, Brooke said, "It's official—Gwen is moving to Oregon. She's leaving this Sunday." This was a turn of events I had hoped would not happen. A few weeks ago, Brooke mentioned that Gwen, her best friend with whom she spent every weekend, might move to Oregon. We were sitting at the kitchen table at the time, having dinner.

I was stunned. "Her whole family is moving? In the middle of the school year?" I had asked at the time.

"No, only her. She'll live with her aunt there."

"Are her parents upset with her? Is there some problem with her living at home?" I questioned.

"I don't know," Brooke said, miserably. "There's not a specific problem. Gwen's siblings went and lived with this aunt when they were in high school. I guess it's a normal thing for them."

"That seems bizarre." I didn't want to sound too judgmental, but I didn't understand why they would do that. It seemed like there had to be a compelling reason. Of course, there could be more to the story than what Brooke knew or wanted to share with me.

"I think her parents are mad that she doesn't want to go to church anymore."

So, there *was* more to the story.

"This aunt is strong in the church, and Gwen's parents think it will be good for her to be around her aunt. She's not that upset about it because she likes her cousins, but I hope she doesn't end up going. I will miss her, and I'll be lonely." I sent a request up to the universe that Gwen would stay here and be with Brooke for the school year.

Now, in the car on the way home from Brooke's doctor appointment, I realized that request was not granted. The sky was gray, and the fall air was crisp and cool. We drove east toward our neighborhood, and that meant driving toward the stately mountains that I never tired of looking at. I asked Brooke, "How do you feel about it?"

"I think it's lame that they're making her go. It didn't have a significant effect on her siblings; half of them don't go to church anymore. I think her parents should accept her for who she is."

"I agree," I responded, inwardly disliking Gwen's parents, whom I had never met. "Do you think you'll be okay?"

"I don't know. I have some other friends, I guess, but no one I like to hang out with as much as her. It's going to be hard."

I nodded in assent. I wasn't a worrier by nature, but I was concerned about how this would affect Brooke. I mentally calculated how long it would be until Thanksgiving or Christmas when Gwen would come home to visit.

"Mom," Brooke interrupted my thoughts, "I wanted to talk to you about another issue. I don't like Sarah, and I want to try a different therapist."

"Okay, we can arrange that. What don't you like about her?" I had spoken with Sarah a few times regarding Brooke's progress or different assignments Sarah had given her. I thought she was fine but nothing outstanding, so I wasn't surprised by Brooke's request.

"She's boring. She doesn't talk, and I don't know what to say to her. I don't feel I'm getting anything out of it."

"Okay, I'll call and get an appointment with someone new when we get home."

No matter how much I didn't want it to happen, Gwen left that Sunday morning. Brooke slept at her house Saturday night, making the most of their diminishing time together. When Brooke came home Sunday morning, I was making crepes for breakfast. Haley was in the kitchen with me. Brooke walked past without saying anything and headed upstairs. Haley and I looked at each other, and Haley said, "I'll go up and see how she's doing."

This was sweet of Haley, but it made me sad because Haley was leaving for her mission in Albuquerque on Tuesday. Why did her departure date have to be so close to when Gwen left? I didn't think Haley leaving would have as great of an effect on Brooke, but it was still unfortunate timing.

Haley came down a few minutes later. "She's upset," she reported. "She cried as she told me about last night and saying goodbye this morning. I'm going to make her a crepe and take it up to her."

The next night, a Monday, Kaitlin and Ben came over for dinner. It was Haley's last night with us, and we wanted to spend it together. I made Hawaiian chicken with coconut rice, one of Haley's favorites, and chocolate chip cookies for dessert. Haley was sad that she would miss out on my homemade chocolate chip cookies for a while, but overall, she was in good spirits. Despite the challenges of participating in long classes over Zoom, Haley had enjoyed her three weeks of preparation. The teachers were engaging, and she had bonded with her fellow trainees. She felt excited and ready to go out and be a missionary.

After dinner, we went downstairs to the basement. We sat around on the stairs, the floor of the landing outside Haley's room, and on the couches in the adjoining family room while Haley packed her last few items. We chatted about this and that and tried not to think about the fact that we wouldn't see Haley for a year and a half.

Bryan took a half day off work to come with me to take Haley to the airport. We had heard that the Covid restrictions required drivers to drop passengers off at the entrance, but we didn't see any signs indicating that. We parked and walked in with her to the security line. She didn't take her personal phone but would be given a phone when she got there. This ensured that the missionaries were on the same phone carrier and enabled the mission leaders to monitor phone usage. Because of that, I wouldn't be able to contact her for a while. Someone would send me a message that she had arrived safely when she got to the mission president's home.

We said our goodbyes, and we both teared up. We hugged tightly and cried hard. I saw an airport official heading my way, presumably telling me that I wasn't supposed to be there, so Bryan and I said a quick "goodbye!" and turned around to head out the door.

The house got a lot quieter after Haley left. I was used to having her around during the day. We had scheduled phone calls with her twice a week, but that wasn't the same as our spontaneous chats while she lived here. I missed sharing the house with another person. Brooke and Sydney had school four days a week by then, but they still got home earlier than usual. This gave the school's janitorial staff time to clean and disinfect each night and limited students' exposure to each other, both of which minimized potential virus spreading. I knew it would be better for them socially and academically to be in school at the regular hours, but I liked having them home more than usual.

A few weeks after Haley left, I went up to Brooke's room in the morning while she was gone. I always walked through her and Sydney's rooms after they left for school to turn off the lights. But this time I had an additional purpose. I looked around, picking up papers and books. I tried not to mess anything up, but I wanted to see if I could find out any inside information about how Brooke was doing. Part of me felt that I shouldn't violate her privacy like this, but another part of me believed that it was a matter of safety. I needed to know if Brooke was struggling more than she was letting on. Teenagers are not known for accurately reporting their mental health. I felt that it was important enough to find out about Brooke's emotional state that I could justify snooping.

I picked up a folded piece of paper and opened it. It was a letter between Brooke and an unknown friend about school and some of their friends, but it was mostly innocuous. I folded it back up and put it in its place. The LED lights on the wall shone green on this day and cycled through changes in intensity, from bright to dim and back to bright again.

I opened a sketch book that sat on the window seat. It was mostly empty, just some drawings on a few of the pages. I looked around her closet, opening drawers and rifling through clothes. I noticed a box on the floor. The shirts hanging above it partially obscured it from view, but I pulled it out and opened it. It was full of folded papers, more notes between friends, cards, and miscellaneous mementos. On top of that was a book with a brown leather cover. As I looked through it, it seemed to be another sketch book, with blank pages instead of lined ones. Most of the pages were empty, but some had sketches, and few more had writing. I read the entries.

It wasn't exactly a journal. There were no dates, and the writings were on random pages, no particular order. At times I had to turn the book upside down to read. Because it wasn't a typical journal, I wasn't sure if the writings were about Brooke's life or stories she had made up. Many of the tales were bizarre or fantastical. Then there would be a rant about someone (unnamed) who spread rumors that she was a slut and how she hated this person. One entry began, "I think I might be a lesbian haha." After reading through the rest of the entry, I remained confused as to whether Brooke was writing about herself or beginning a fictional story.

I was mildly concerned about what I read, but also knew that these outbursts were normal for teenagers. One part of me was glad that she had this creative outlet to channel her frustrations, whether real or made up. I didn't find anything that I felt I needed to confront Brooke about, nothing urgently dangerous. But it gave me a general idea of where she was at. There were entries about witchcraft and Tarot cards, girls that she never wanted to speak to again, and days when she tried to limit herself to 500 calories (again, fact or fiction?). I stored these ideas away in my head and made plans to bring them up casually. For example, a few weeks later I said, "I know a lot of girls don't like the way they look and try to lose weight. Have you ever tried to limit your food?" She said no. I explored a little more, but nothing came of it.

I wasn't surprised by the references to witchcraft. Brooke had mentioned this to us before, in a half-joking way. I already sensed that Brooke wasn't interested in the church. She never complained or asked to stay home from church meetings, though. Every Wednesday night, the young women aged twelve to eighteen got together for activities. Brooke occasionally asked to skip these but more because she didn't like the girls than because she didn't like the church teachings. Nothing specific was written in the book about the church, but I had my suspicions confirmed that she was not the usual Christian "good girl." This didn't bother me, though. I was almost relieved. I was contemplating leaving the church anyway, and this meant one fewer child to disappoint or confuse.

Another reason I was looking around Brooke's room was to find clues about her and Sam's relationship. The Friday before Halloween, Sam had taken Brooke on their first official date.

Brooke seemed flattered and excited to go. I wanted to know if there was anything more going on that she hadn't talked about. I did not have any concerns about Sam. He continued to be a wonderful guy—friendly and thoughtful and fun to be with. Sam's parents intrigued me. They were members of our church but seemed to have a liberal streak. They both did graduate work at UC Berkeley, and both worked as university professors in the humanities field. Their political leanings and the fact that his mother had a career were unusual for our religion.

Brooke told me they had a yard sign that was also uncommon for members of our church and families in our area. It said, "WE BELIEVE" at the top and then had a list of statements like "BLACK LIVES MATTER," "LOVE IS LOVE," and "SCIENCE IS REAL." This was ironic because our religion has thirteen Articles of Faith, each of which starts with "We believe." This yard sign seemed almost like a reference to that, but indicated that they believe in secular philosophies, too. When Brooke mentioned this sign, I wanted one for our yard. I loved so much about it: the acceptance of gay love or any other kind love, the assertion that Black lives matter, and the proclamation that science is real, which in this moment meant that the Covid virus is what the scientists say it is and that we should wear masks to protect ourselves and others and get the vaccine once it becomes available.

I ordered one of these yard signs the night Brooke told me about Sam's and put it out as soon as it came. I would have been more nervous to make these declarations if I didn't know that Sam's parents also had this sign. Even with their example, I felt uneasy about what my neighbors might think. Displaying this sign was a signal to myself and my community that maybe I was willing to put other ideas above some of our religious teachings. I was both excited and anxious: I want this to be who I am, but am I really this person? This is what I believe; do I dare be authentic?

In the notes and writings I found in Brooke's room that day, there was no direct reference to Sam, Gwen leaving, or her mental health, specifically. It was useful for me, however, to get a better sense of what went on in her mind. I now knew that she might be lesbian or bisexual. It was nice to have some time to get used to that idea before she came out to us. I told Bryan what I had read and found in her room. He took it in stride, as he usually does. We both agreed that it's maybe not what we would have hoped and dreamed for her, but it was going to be all right.

CHAPTER 6

The Stories in My Head

One afternoon when I was about nine years old, my mom asked me if I wanted to go to the store with her. I didn't have anything to do and thought it would be fun to go, but I was mad at my mom about something. I let the irritation override the desire to go and told her no, I didn't want to. She said "fine" and got in the car. I kneeled backwards on the living room couch, facing the large windows that looked out over the front yard, and watched her pull out and drive away. Suddenly my body filled with regret, and I started to whimper, "I want to go." Tears formed in my eyes as I thought about how I had made the wrong choice. I stayed on that couch for the better part of an hour, getting more and more worked up. The "I want to go" refrain went from a moan to a sob to a shriek. I cried harder and harder until my eyes were red and stinging.

A few years later, we went on a family vacation to Washington, D.C. As we toured the White House, we learned that President Reagan would be leaving soon, and if we stood on the south lawn, we could watch the motorcade pull out and drive away. Everyone was excited about this unusual opportunity to be so close to the president. We went outside, found the crowd, and waited along with them. It must've taken a long time because I got bored and wanted to leave. I asked if we could go, but my parents wanted to stay to see the procession.

I got fidgety and tired of standing and decided to wander off. My parents called out to me to not go too far, or I would miss it. I walked up the sidewalk to where the crowd ended and kept going. I felt angry and annoyed and didn't care about seeing the president. Nobody was listening to me and my wants. When I was about a block away, I heard cheering and clapping. I looked back toward the crowd. I figured the black SUVs that made up the motorcade were streaming by, but I couldn't see the street or any cars because of the crowd. I walked back toward my family, but by the time I got there, everything was over.

"You missed it," my mom said, as if it wasn't obvious. I was angry at myself. Why did I walk away? Why did I let the boredom and irritation get the best of me? I stayed mad the rest of the day, and my parents were frustrated with my mood and behavior. My mom pulled me aside angrily and said, "You're ruining the trip. Don't be a martyr." I wasn't sure what a martyr was, but I got the idea: stop feeling sorry for yourself. She said that command, "Don't be a martyr," to me many times throughout the years, most often on trips, and she also frequently admonished me to "change your attitude."

These and other similar events in my childhood created a story in my mind that I am a negative person, a sulky girl who feels sorry for herself too often and too easily. I worked hard throughout my teenage years to be more positive, and I succeeded on some level. In the years following, it wasn't uncommon for people to point out my positivity and enthusiasm for the joys of life. But deep down I knew the truth—I was a negative person putting on a show. I never believed their compliments. I looked back on these childhood incidents with regret and disdain. I didn't like myself because of my pessimistic outlook on life.

Throughout my life, I continued to struggle on vacations. When Bryan was in medical school and residency, we didn't go on many trips besides home to see our families, so I don't remember any negative experiences. However, when he finished residency, we had more money to travel. Most people assume that you *want* to go on more vacations, as many as you can afford. The kids were older and easier to leave; this was supposed to be the fun time of life with a multitude of couples and family trips. But I was often grumpy wherever we went. I thought the trips sounded fun when we planned them, but when I was actually on them, I reverted to my negative attitude. I felt horrible that I couldn't just be happy. I had a wonderful husband, four great kids, and enough money to travel to exciting places. I didn't find them exciting, though; I was miserable. I didn't let on how unhappy I felt. I tried to put on a positive face. Sometimes the emotional pain would break through, and I would end up showing my frustration and occasionally crying. The more trips we went on, the more frequently this happened.

When we weren't traveling, I could manage my emotions better. I felt confident in my role as homemaker, household manager, and mother; therefore, I didn't have as many negative thoughts about myself when I was home. After I turned forty, however, the pessimism spread to other areas of my life.

During this time, certain parts of my life created more frequent discontent. I had always felt like I didn't fit in with my family, because I was the only religious one. I thought I would be happier in a different situation, and this belief strengthened over the years. I found it harder and harder to interact with my family, whether on vacations to visit them or over the phone. Also, many of my friends moved away at this time. I started to feel disappointed in my social life. Furthermore, my kids were getting older, and I didn't have a plan for what to do with my time once they all went to school. I had looked forward to having kid-free time and made a conscious decision to not commit myself to anything else (like serving as PTA president or tackling some home makeover project). But when the time came, I found the long hours in the empty house lonely and unsatisfying.

In my estimation, I had a lot of reasons to feel sorry for myself. When I was down, I mentally listed them and wallowed in self-pity. But I also felt angry and annoyed with myself. I had a great life! Why was I complaining? I had a kind and loving husband, kids who were obedient and successful at school, a nice house, and the leisure to choose what I wanted to do each day. Why was I sad and despondent?

Some people call this a midlife crisis, but researchers have discovered a different, more nuanced phenomenon labeled the U-curve of happiness. When they combined the results of happiness surveys from all ages and all over the world, with mood on the vertical axis and age on the horizontal one, the data points form a U-shaped line. The bottom of the U is at approximately age fifty. Bryan and I learned about this from his brother and sister-in-law, Mike and Josie. It came up as we ate dinner together at our favorite Indian restaurant in our hometown. We had coordinated our trips back home for a summer vacation so that we could spend time together. When they told us about this concept over our chicken tikka masala, it seared into my brain and immediately made sense to me. Later I looked up the graph for myself and read some articles about it.

People think that the hard part of adulthood and parenting is when your kids are young. Their needs are relentless, and you have little freedom. It is equally logical to assume that the early years of your career will be the most difficult. But, in fact, the opposite is true. The toil and strain of those years brings a certain kind of satisfaction, or maybe you don't have time to deal with your stressful feelings, and you stuff them down. When you get into your forties, you have more space to feel those emotions and examine your life. Your kids take less work and the demands of your job start to level out. Around this time, you realize that maybe this is as good as life gets. You're never going to get the promotion you've been working so hard for, or your marriage is never going to be what you'd hoped and envisioned, despite your efforts. Your kids become teenagers and begin making their own choices, and you realize that your dream of what they'll become that you've been able to sustain over the years is crumbling. Most people have one of these dynamics, if not multiple.

Understanding this idea gave me some comfort. It was nice to know that other people went through the same feelings, and I gained comfort when I saw that most people get happier as the arrow of time goes on. But it didn't alleviate all my current pain. I still felt increasingly distressed, and my crying episodes became more frequent.

My brain was on the lookout for a solution to this problem, so when I heard about a book called *Feeling Good* by David Burns, I was intrigued. I borrowed a copy from the library but soon decided to purchase my own copy to write notes in the margins and fold down the corners of interesting pages. David Burns is one of the pioneers of cognitive therapy, which holds the principle that our thoughts create our feelings. The book described how to become aware of thoughts and identify the "thinking errors" in them that generate emotional pain. Thinking errors included all-or-nothing thinking, maximizing and minimizing, mind-reading, overgeneralization, and labelling. We can reframe the erroneous thoughts into "rational responses," something more compassionate and reasonable.[16]

I took notes on the various thinking errors and began to journal about my thoughts and identify the inaccuracies. I gained a lot of insight into my thought patterns through this process. The vignette examples in the book fascinated me, and I loved seeing how quickly Dr. Burns' patients felt better. I related to their pain, especially when they described how they didn't have anything "real" to complain about. I spent a lot of time writing about my problems and what thoughts I had surrounding them. Sometimes I felt self-indulgent spending time on this; I worried that I might reinforce the negative thoughts by concentrating on them. But the book assured me that awareness was an important first step.

There were other helpful strategies in Dr. Burns' book, and I worked hard to implement them. The principles gave me consolation for a time, but I could not fully alleviate the pain from my thoughts, even when I recognized them as errors. I went through cycles in those years of sensing mounting depression and getting so helpless and hopeless that I contemplated going on antidepressant medication. Then things would get a little better and I would feel okay for a few months.

During a downturn in one of those cycles, I heard about a life coach podcast. I dismissed it at first, but after someone else mentioned it to me, I thought I might as well try it out. I had low expectations. I didn't think anything could help me get out of my funk. The coach, Liz, called herself a thought work coach to distinguish herself from life coaches who focus primarily on setting and achieving goals. The podcast was intriguing; it started with the premise of cognitive therapy (Liz taught that all problems are thought problems) but went a lot further. I liked what I heard, and I wanted to learn more.

On August 2, 2018, I joined a call to hear a more detailed description of Liz's online program. She explained that once enrolled in the program, members can get coached by her over Zoom. Other members listen to the coaching live or access the recording later. Listening to people get coached is powerful, Liz said; hearing others work through their thoughts helps loosen stuck ideas in your brain even more than getting direct help. The program also included monthly classes and an online chat feature.

After the explanation, Liz brought on volunteers and talked through their problems. Having a glimpse into other people's lives and problems fascinated me, and the way Liz talked them through the dilemma and helped them see it in a new way was captivating. I felt like this was different, something that could really help me. I joined that day.[17]

As I had with the *Feeling Good* book, I worked hard to learn, study, and implement the new material. I spent hours listening to classes and coaching calls and writing about my problems and my thoughts regarding them. Some people might need more individualized help, but my personality was perfect for the independent study style of this program. Even though I'd heard of some of the concepts before, the way Liz taught enabled them to sink in and profoundly change the way I think. I had impressive breakthroughs right away. I began to understand my depression, and most importantly, how to combat it.

One of the first things I learned that gave me solace was this fact: human brains continuously scan for problems. This answers my burning question, "Why am I miserable when I have so many great things in my life?" Our human brains are wired to inspect our lives, ourselves, and other people for shortcomings and missed expectations and find them. No matter what our circumstances, the brain will eventually find something to be upset about. Whether the problem is lack of access to clean water or a dishwasher that continually breaks, it doesn't matter. The psychic pain caused by the brain when it believes something has gone wrong is the same. This meant that I could stop feeling guilty for being sad. It's okay that I'm gloomy; this is what humans do. We create negative emotions for ourselves, and we always will. There's no getting around it.

Furthermore, when the scanner in our brain finds something wrong, our powerful brains work to make that idea true. You act in ways that reinforce your beliefs, and you look for evidence that your belief is correct. Part of this is confirmation bias—we focus on things that support our opinions and disregard experiences that don't—but it goes further than that. It sounds crazy, but your actions change to create a result that fits with the thoughts, even when the thoughts center on what you *don't* want in your life. When I held the view that I lacked friends, I often noticed other people's large friend groups, I discounted people who reached out to me, and I acted bothered and standoffish in social situations. I unwittingly constructed a situation that matched my theory. We do this even though it causes pain for ourselves. Our brain focuses more on being right and making its claims come true than on bringing us happiness.

Some people find the next idea I learned challenging, but I found great comfort when I chose to believe that whatever happens is supposed to happen. When you accept what happens in your life instead of fighting against it, you have more serenity and more problem-solving ability. Our natural inclination is to see two paths: be angry and do something about the problem *or* be at peace and don't work to change things. However, those are not the only options. You can be peaceful and accept your reality while still working to change it. The brain thinks that anger and resentment are useful emotions; the brain says we need to feel those emotions to be effective. This is not true. Indeed, the calmer you remain, the more successfully you will navigate your life.

Byron Katie talks about this in her amazing book, *Loving What Is: Four Questions That Can Change Your Life.* She writes, "When you argue with reality you will lose, but only every time."[18] On the other hand, to allow what is happening and stop resisting it brings tranquility. When you believe that everything happens as it is supposed to, it takes away your apprehension about the future and your regrets about the past. It removes any frustration about how your life is going right now. It's all as it's supposed to be.

When I adopted this tenet, it helped me let go of my worries about how my kids would turn out. In our church, we were taught that the most important thing is to stay on the path of righteousness. Doing the things that would keep you on this path not only led to eternal salvation, but also comprised the only way to find happiness in this life. Both these concepts create a lot of pressure on families for their kids to act a certain way and follow a particular life course. Bryan and I worried that our kids wouldn't follow the church teachings and conform to that way of life. We feared that they would have difficulties in life because of that, but more honestly, we were apprehensive that our family wouldn't look the way we wanted it to. We had an idea of how our family should appear, and we felt anything else would be subpar.

Some of our children already didn't fit that vision, however. I felt consoled when I adopted the belief that nothing has gone wrong with our kids. Things will always go as they are supposed to, so we don't need to fear. In fact, even the notion that one way to live is better than another is a story. Circumstances are neutral until we think a thought about it. Our brains gather ideas and opinions throughout our lives from our families, from society, and from our genetic makeup. Sometimes we latch onto these theories as Truth, even when they cause us pain. Stories like kids should stay in the church or my life should be different are weapons we use to create negative emotion for ourselves. Then our brains go to work to make that idea come true, even though it is what we don't want.

When I learned this, I thought of my perception of myself as a negative person. My brain had latched onto the experiences I had as a child and made up this opinion. Then it scanned for evidence. It noticed and catalogued times when I wasn't happy, and it disregarded times when I was. Remember the friends who complimented me on my positive attitude? My brain would not accept that as accurate because it wanted to hold on to the other story. The truth is I was just a kid; I was a human trying to feel good in the world. I did the best that I could. I had times where I was negative and times where I was enthusiastic and positive. There is nothing wrong with how I was then or how I am now. What a relief!

I also examined my belief that enjoying vacations was better than not liking them. That was another story I created, latched onto, and used to punish myself. Apparently, this is how I was supposed to be. I was intended to feel mediocre about vacations. I was meant to be grumpy while there. That was okay. Once I started to accept this (I'm still working on it), vacations got more enjoyable. I realized that I brought a mean lady along with me on vacation who told me continuously how I was negative and boring. Who would want to go on vacation if you had to be with her? I could attempt to convince myself that I loved vacations, but it was much more powerful to accept that it was *okay* that I didn't like them. I tried out new thoughts such as, "You shouldn't be any different than you are," and "You're doing a great job. This is hard, but you showed up, and that's amazing." Also, "It's okay to feel negative emotion. Your brain thinks it's a tragedy but it's not; this is what it's like to be human."

Allowing emotions is another crucial part of feeling good. Contrary to our natural inclinations, it's okay to have negative emotions. They aren't as dangerous as our brains tell us, and we'll never get rid of them completely. This was a revelation to me. I was convinced that my sadness and frustration indicated that something was wrong with me or with my life. As I unraveled that belief and gave myself space to allow and process my negative feelings, I felt much better. I eventually came to accept that all emotions, even self-dislike (the scariest emotion for me), were permitted. The best counsel Liz gave me was when she said, "What if you said yes to your frustration, yes to your tears, yes to your discontent? It's all part of the human experience. Don't resist it. Allow it."

This is not what you expect from a life coach. You anticipate that she will teach you how to escape negative emotion. But Liz communicated time and again that it's normal and unavoidable to feel the whole range of emotions. Negative feelings are not pleasant, but they are not dangerous. Our brain goes into overdrive trying to resist them. But when we relax and allow them, they move through us more easily.

This type of coaching is like cognitive therapy with a Zen addition. We acknowledge that our thoughts create our negative feelings but grant that we'll never get rid of those difficult emotions completely. When you accept that life is painful, you suffer less.

Another Zen aspect of thought-work coaching gets back to the idea that everything that happens is supposed to happen. Another way of saying this is "the universe is constantly conspiring in my favor." When you choose to believe that everything happens *for* you instead of *to* you, you gain leverage over the situation and have a great vantage point from which to solve your problems.

Christians talk about faith and say that they believe in an omniscient God, but when one of their children leaves the church or they have some other trial in life, they are quick to conclude that something has gone "wrong." It's as if they think God looked away for a minute and let this unfortunate thing happen. When you truly believe that God knows what He is sending you and what experiences you need, you approach life differently. You accept what comes into your life and ask God how to deal with it instead of asking why this is happening. Christians have a strong belief that there is one right way for everyone to live life and anything else is problematic. Because of this, they sometimes struggle to allow whatever God sends them. They have trouble letting others be who they are and try out different ways of living. They react to "sinful" people with either disapproval or fear, not with acceptance or curiosity.

As I learned about coaching and thought work and applied the principles in my life, I began to feel better. It was comforting to let go of the impression of myself as an inherently negative person. I started to enjoy vacations more by taking a kinder approach in my self-talk. When I felt upset, I practiced becoming aware of my thoughts and gently reminding myself that they were not true, simply stories my brain came up with. I learned to not judge myself for creating and believing these stories. Criticizing them makes them go back into hiding. I let them come up and get some air. I metaphorically put them out on the table to assess them and their effect and decide if they are serving me or not.

For me, this approach to problematic thoughts was more powerful than positive affirmations. I had used positive affirmations in the past with some success. In the early stages of parenting, I was impatient and angry with my toddlers. I found a self-help book that taught me how to use affirmations, and I repeated them religiously for ten years. When my new set of problems cropped up, however, positive affirmations seemed too weak to conquer them. Coaching taught me a different method. Now when I found a story that caused me pain (such as, "I don't fit in with my family") instead of turning that around ("I fit perfectly with my family") and trying to convince myself the positive statement was true, I went deeper. I questioned the whole premise. Who says being the same as your family is better than being different? Your brain tells you happiness comes from being the same, but it's possible that's not true; it's possible you'd be more unhappy. How do I feel and act when I believe the thought, "I don't fit in with my family"? Is that thought serving me? What do other people in my situation think? How much would we have to have in common for me to fit in? I took the story apart and saw it for what it was. When I did that, the painful narrative melted away.

These new ideas provided a more peaceful way to think about myself and my life. I wasn't perfect at assessing my thoughts or feeling my feelings, and I still had a lot of negative emotion. But when I struggled, I had a framework to go to; I understood why and what to do about it; I had a process to guide me through the thoughts and feelings and help me work them out.

Learning about coaching also confirmed some of my recent thoughts about my church. The church teaches there's one right way to live your life (and that way looks a lot like white culture). It tells me to force my kids into living this way or something has gone horribly wrong. When I looked at those past ideas with my new perspective, they seemed narrow-minded and full of unnecessary alarm. I no longer believed that one way to live was better than another. I now knew that these were stories we came up with as humans and held onto, even when they didn't serve us.

CHAPTER 7

"I Can't Do This Anymore"

It was a normal Sunday, like so many others. We slept in and lazily got ready for church, which began at noon. Even though Covid numbers were rising, our congregation had decided to allow a small, rotating number of people to attend in-person services each week. They broadcasted the services over YouTube for the others to watch. This Sunday, November 15, 2020, it was our turn to go to live church. We dressed in our Sunday best. Brooke, Sydney, and I wore dresses, and Bryan looked handsome in his suit and tie. Sydney asked if she could wear her Nike Air Forces with her dress.

I said no, those were not appropriate shoes for church. The pink in Brooke's hair had faded and was barely noticeable.

After church, we changed back into casual clothes. I read some, and the girls watched TV. At four p.m., I started preparing dinner; at five p.m., Kaitlin and Ben came over to eat with us. We were still not used to Haley being gone. The dining room table seemed empty without her. After dinner, Brooke and Sydney went to the gray couches while Kaitlin, Ben, Bryan, and I discussed current events. Brooke had seemed quiet all day. I watched her, curled up on the couch, scrolling through her phone, and had a small ache of worry. The first term of the school year had recently ended. Brooke's grades turned out decent but not as good as usual. She had especially struggled in English. She didn't finish assignments and sometimes didn't even turn in completed work. She said she didn't have the energy or concentration, and she complained about having three days a week of online school. But even when in person school went to from two to four days a week, her work didn't improve.

Later in the evening, Sydney wanted to show Kaitlin and Ben something in her room. They went upstairs and ended up sitting around chatting. Brooke was in her room next door, and Kaitlin went in to talk to her and try to include her in the conversation. I walked by and heard Kaitlin say, "Your room is so clean!" I went in to see. Brooke's bed was made, her books and computer piled neatly against the wall. She had cleared the books and scraps of paper off her window seat. The trinkets on her shelves were organized and straightened. And the clothes in her closet were hung up tidily. I complimented her on her hard work.

I walked into the laundry room and got another surprise. We had designated a desk area in one corner of this room Brooke's atelier. Her paints, brushes, notepads, and markers were usually strewn across the counter. Clear plastic protected the desk and was smudged with numerous drops and blotches of paint. But today everything was neat. The desk was uncluttered; supplies were organized in bins or put away in the cupboards. I went back to Brooke's room and gave her a hug. "Thanks for cleaning that up. It looks lovely!" Brooke smiled and nodded. By the next day, I knew that this urge to organize was more ominous than magnanimous.

At 10:30 that night, Bryan and I headed to bed. We locked the front door, turned off most of the lights, and said good night to Brooke. Sydney had gone to bed about an hour before. Brooke was in the kitchen having a snack. We asked her to turn off the lights when she went to bed. By eleven p.m., Bryan and I were asleep.

Shortly after midnight, I awakened. At first, I was disoriented, but then I saw light coming from my phone on the nightstand. I picked up the phone. The call was not from someone in my contacts, but the area code was local, so I answered it.

"Hello."

"Is this Brooke's mom?" The voice sounded timid and shaken.

"Yes." I started to get out of bed. Somehow, I knew where this was going.

"This is Anna, Brooke's friend. She has taken some pills. Can you check on her?"

I don't know what else she said because I cut her off. My

stomach had gone cold, and there was a faint buzzing in my head. I said, "Yes, thank you for calling," and hung up. By this time, I was out of bed and heading for the door. I put the phone down on the chest of drawers. Bryan had woken up and asked, "What's happening?"

I barely turned around. I was groping in the dark for the door handle as I said, "Brooke's taken something. We need to go to her." He jumped up and followed me. We walked the short distance down the hall to her room. Before I opened the door, I saw the cool-blue LED light coming from underneath. That color—added to the late hour—lent an eerie quality to the hallway. I didn't stop to brace myself. I didn't know what I would find on the other side of that door, but I didn't hesitate to walk in.

Once in the room, I could see clearly because of the LED lights. Her bed was empty. I walked over to the space between the bed and the window seat. Brooke's electric guitar leaned against the wall next to an amp. She'd asked for those for her birthday earlier this year and had taken lessons over the summer. She enjoyed it, but then she became too depressed to focus on it or improve. On the floor in front of the amp were an empty pill bottle plus three envelopes addressed with names, all lined up neatly. One said, "mom and dad," one said, "Sam," and one said, "Gwen Hughes" and had Gwen's address in Oregon below the name and a stamp in the corner. Sam's was on top of a neatly folded sweatshirt, one of his that Brooke had borrowed. Next to Gwen's was a Build-a-Bear stuffed animal that they had purchased together.

My eyes quickly grazed over the letters and other items as I knelt to get closer to Brooke. She sat on the floor, slumped against the built-in drawers under the bed, head back, eyes looking off in the distance, arms lifeless against her sides. She had on a t-shirt and sweatpants. The white earbuds in her ears connected via slim white wires to her phone, which she held in her hand. I searched her face for clues. A wave of relief washed over me when I realized she was conscious and awake. She seemed dazed and started to shake her head when she saw us.

"Brooke! Are you okay?"

She nodded but looked miserable. Her face was pale and drawn. I had that preternatural calm that comes over me in major crises. As soon as I saw that she was conscious, I understood everything would be okay. Bryan had followed me in and sat on the bed looking down. I knew he could save Brooke if there was a medical problem between now and when we got to the hospital. Bryan is a trained anesthesiologist as well as a spine interventionalist. For ten years, he worked 80 percent of his time in a pain clinic and 20 percent in a hospital doing obstetric and general anesthesia. Anesthesiologists are the life savers. They are the most skilled at clearing airways and helping patients breathe. They run the codes at the hospital. We were safe.

I also knew that we'd have a big ordeal ahead of us. Thanks to my clinical therapy training and Bryan's medical background, we had an inkling of what would happen next and what we needed to do to help Brooke get over this and feel whole again. I metaphorically took a deep breath and jumped in. *Let's do it.*

It had only been a few seconds since we'd entered the room. I picked up Brooke's phone and looked at it. The screen showed a text conversation, and the green phone call icon was in the corner. I asked Brooke whom she was talking to; she said Gwen. I asked her to say goodbye. In a quiet and choked voice she told Gwen her parents were here, and she had to go.

I said something like, "What happened?" Brooke held up the pill bottle and said, "I took them." She began to cry. I took the bottle from her and saw that it was her antidepressant medication, duloxetine (Cymbalta). I found the date it was filled, November 7, 2020, and the quantity: 30 pills. That means there were more than twenty pills left in the bottle. I also saw the packaging of Nyquil tablets lying next to her. It had held eight pills and they were all gone. I handed the pill bottle and the Nyquil packaging to Bryan then looked back at Brooke. Silent tears rolled down her face. I leaned toward her and rubbed her leg.

She said, "I can't do it anymore. It's so painful. I can't do it."

I asked, "What is so painful?" I wasn't sure if she had some physical pain.

She seemed exasperated. She let out a huff and said, "I don't know. This," her arms gestured around the room weakly. "Life. It's too hard. I can't do it."

I rubbed her leg methodically and tried to soothe her by saying, "I know. It's okay. It's going to be okay."

Bryan had left the room and came back with his phone in his hand. He had dialed Poison Control and was waiting for someone to answer. I was thankful for him and his ability to handle any medical situation. It had always been such a benefit to our family and a relief in stressful times.

Poison Control answered and Bryan walked to the hall again as he explained what had happened. I heard him calmly say the name of the medication and how many pills were missing. He also told them about the Nyquil tablets. He walked back in the room as he hung up the phone.

"We need to take her to the ER. They will call ahead and tell the ER what happened and what course of action they suggest."

"Isn't that something the ER should know?" I questioned.

Bryan said, "There are so many different medications people take, it's difficult to know the details about all of them. Poison Control is the expert, so ERs rely on them."

We looked at Brooke and took a pause to let it sink in. We asked Brooke if she thought she could walk, and she nodded her head. When she stood up, I gave her a big hug and told her I loved her. Bryan did the same. He helped her downstairs and to the car. I went to our bedroom closet and changed from pajamas to jeans and a t-shirt. Bryan had already dressed.

The car ride to the ER was silent. The black asphalt of the streets shone under the streetlights and stoplights. I didn't know if I should be talking to Brooke, calming her, or asking more questions about her state of mind. How would anyone know what to do in this situation? I had grabbed the letters Brooke left out to read later and maybe to give to the crisis counselor. I also brought Brooke's phone. We had decided that Sydney would be okay by herself at home, even though we had no idea when we'd be back.

As we walked toward the bright lights of the ER entrance, we each put on a mask. I was numb, unsure how sick Brooke would be and what the hospital experience would be like. We spoke to the nurse at the reception desk and then sat down. The waiting room was mostly empty. Two or three people had checked in before us; we sat quietly until Brooke's name was called. After a short while, a nurse led us through the double doors and past the nurses' station to a dimly lit room. She had Brooke change into a hospital gown and then hooked her up to an array of monitors. Bryan pointed out with concern that her heart rate was extremely elevated and that her blood pressure was high.

After the nurse finished the preparations and left, we were alone in the room for a while, Brooke on the hospital bed and Bryan and me in chairs next to her. She was not asleep but looked away from us. While we waited, we opened Brooke's phone and looked through it. We couldn't find anything of interest in the Notes or Photos apps. We read the recent text conversation between her and Gwen. Around 11:45 p.m., Brooke had texted, "I took them. I'm sorry." Gwen must have called right after that and kept her on the line. I figured Gwen notified Anna and asked her to phone us. I felt horrible that Gwen had to go through that but also overwhelmingly grateful that she knew what to do.

We opened Brooke's Safari app and clicked on the browsing history. Our stomachs dropped as we looked through her searches. "How fatal is duloxetine?" "How many antidepressant pills do I need to take to die?" "Are SSRIs lethal?" The websites that popped up from these searches said that yes, those pills are lethal if you take enough. My tears started flowing freely. I had trouble catching my breath. I stepped out of the room, and Bryan followed me.

I calmed down enough to ask Bryan, "Is this true? Are they deadly? You don't hear about people dying from an overdose of antidepressants." He said he didn't think they were that dangerous. He expected they would monitor Brooke for possible adverse effects, but she would not have long-term harm. We went back to the room and sat again.

Finally, the nurse came in and asked us to recount what had happened. Soon after that, the doctor came in, and we told the story again. They took blood from Brooke's arm to run some tests. Then they asked us to go to a family waiting room while the crisis counselor talked to Brooke alone for a bit. The nurse led us to the room and said the counselor would come in after he spoke with Brooke.

In the quiet after the nurse left, I remembered the letters Brooke had written. I got them out and read through them. They were heartbreaking. Each was a single page, written in pink pen on cream-colored paper that had been ripped out of a journal. Although the three letters were similar, Gwen's was the longest and most plaintive. It said in part,

> i'm so incredibly sorry. theres so many things i want you to know. youve been the most amazing person in my life. you brought so much happiness & you are truly the reason i fought for so long. i never wanted to hurt you, but i can't do this anymore. please understand how badly I want to stay for you, but everything else is too much. im sorry im not enough. im sorry im not strong enough & i can't keep fighting. you're the strongest best person i know. you changed my life. please please be OK. please keep fighting. don't mourn me & just forget me. im so so so sorry. i love you so much. i need you to know this wasn't your fault, you did everything you could...

It went on for a while longer, repeating similar phrases and imploring Gwen to keep fighting, stay safe, get the help she needs. Again and again, she said how sorry she was and how she couldn't do it anymore. It ended with:

> i know this letter isn't enough & doesn't make up for what I've done, but you have so much left to do here. my time was up, but you have a beautiful life ahead. i love you.

Reading these letters added to the dreamlike feeling of the whole night. Were we truly here, at the ER, reading suicide notes from our daughter? It was unreal. My emotions vacillated between anguish caused by the letters to tremendous gratitude that she wasn't gone. Bryan and I looked at each other but didn't know what to say.

Eventually, the crisis counselor came into the room. He wore black scrubs, as opposed to the blue and light blue scrubs of the medical team. He was in his late twenties, tall and strongly built, and had a beard. As we spoke, he could see the tears welling up in my eyes, but I was thankful my mask concealed my constant chin quivering and lip pursing. The taut calm I'd felt up until that point gave way to fear and embarrassment. I didn't want to talk to this person about my child's depression and suicide attempt. I wanted to be a normal, happy family whose kids smiled a lot and had enough energy to be on the dance team or join the debate club.

The counselor began with how sorry he was that we found ourselves in this position. He reassured us he'd seen many families like ours and that everything would be okay. He was kind, matter of fact, and professional, but my mind couldn't concentrate on what he said. It kept jumping to questions such as, what's going to happen to her? What does this mean for her future? How long will she stay in the hospital and where will she go after that? I asked him these questions and more. He tried to answer them, but there were many things he didn't know or couldn't predict. He said most people go from the emergency room or hospital stay to an inpatient behavioral unit (or "psych ward," as we used to call it). It was his job to help us find such a placement for Brooke. The units were quite busy, he explained, because of escalating mental health problems resulting from Covid-induced isolation and fear. He hoped we could find a spot for Brooke by the time she was discharged, but otherwise we'd have to take her home. That thought frightened and overwhelmed me. How would I interact with her and keep her safe after this experience? I pushed the idea out of my mind.

The counselor told us that when he talked to Brooke, she didn't mention any specific grievances with her family. That was a relief. He said she felt overwhelmed with school and friends and didn't think she could handle living life anymore. When he questioned us about her behavior at home, we described how she was lethargic and melancholy but not defiant or difficult. We showed him the search history on her phone and told him about the letters.

He looked directly at us and said, "This was a serious attempt." My heart skipped a beat, and I gave him my full attention. He continued, "She took the whole bottle." He let that sink in. "I've seen many kids here and not all of them are as thorough as she was, with the letters and the research and the timing. The fact that she emptied her bottle of pills and took the NyQuil on top of that shows in what a dark and desperate place she was."

Suddenly, I thought of how she'd cleaned her room and organized her art desk earlier that day. My body clenched as I realized she had been planning and preparing all day, maybe even for longer. Thank heaven she reached out to Gwen after taking the pills. How lucky we were that she had such a good friend whom she trusted enough to call, and that Gwen was available and quick-thinking. This was a horrible situation to be in, but things could be worse. I relaxed somewhat knowing that we were lucky; we still had her, we could get help and work on this problem, and have a future with Brooke in it.

After speaking with us a little longer, the counselor left to write his report. He said the nurse would be back to get us shortly. Bryan and I looked at the clock, it was after one a.m. We realized we needed to make plans for Sydney for the next day and what Bryan should do about work. Thanks to Bryan's good health and immense work ethic, he had never missed a day of work. Occasionally he got a cold, but he always slogged through it. He had over thirty patients scheduled for the next day; he couldn't not show up. One of the patients had been off his blood thinners over the weekend to prepare for his procedure on Monday. It would be dangerous to delay it.

This was the gravest thing that had ever happened to our family. We were not used to family crises disrupting Bryan's schedule. I couldn't handle the next day alone, though. Obviously, I relied on Bryan's medical knowledge and opinions. I needed him there for the vital conversations and decisions. We talked it over and decided that he would go in to do the hour-long procedure on the patient who couldn't wait. The rest of the patients would be rescheduled for future dates or added onto his partner's schedule. This created a lot of work for the office, but the situation necessitated it.

We moved on to discuss what to do about Sydney. This brought Kaitlin and Ben to mind—maybe Sydney could go to their house tomorrow. When I thought about them, it occurred to me that Ben might still be awake. Kaitlin went to bed between nine and ten, but Ben often stayed up later. I wanted to talk to him immediately. I texted him, "Are you awake?" Bryan and I stared at the phone for a few strained minutes. We could see he was typing and finally the reply came, "Yeah, what's up?"

I touched the phone icon, and Ben answered right away. Telling our kids was one of the worst parts of this ordeal for me. It was awful sharing this painful news, knowing how it would affect them, their mental health, and their overall lives.

I began to say, "Ben, we're in the hospital." My throat constricted and my voice choked. He was worried. "What's happening?" he asked. I tried to get more words out, but they ended up in a sob. Bryan took the phone from me. Tears were coming down his face, but he could speak with more composure.

Bryan said, "It's Brooke. She's taken some pills. It was an attempt..." he couldn't get the words out. Ben seemed frantic, "What should I do? Should I go get Kaitlin up? I'll go get Kaitlin." Moments passed and then Kaitlin's voice came on, soft and groggy. Bryan explained what had happened. Kaitlin started crying, and we could hear quiet sniffles from Ben, also. We talked for a bit about what the counselor had said and what might happen next. We asked them if Sydney could come to their house the next day while we stayed in the hospital. They readily agreed, and we said we'd talk again in the morning.

After hanging up with Ben and Kaitlin, it took me a while to calm down. When I did, Bryan and I further discussed our plans. We decided that he should go home to sleep and be there when Sydney woke up. Besides, there was only one comfortable chair in Brooke's ER room. We wiped our eyes and blew our noses while we waited for the nurse to return. After a short time, she came into the room, followed by the doctor. The blood work had come back, the doctor said, and Brooke was going to be okay. Because of the number of pills she took, she had what was called serotonin syndrome. An overdose of SSRIs can increase blood levels of serotonin, causing a cluster of symptoms including high blood pressure, high body temperature, and increased heart rate, as well as agitation, tremors, and possibly seizures.

The doctor said that Brooke seemed fine right now. Her heart rate and blood pressure were elevated, and they would keep an eye on that, but she didn't have any other symptoms currently. Serotonin syndrome can be lethal, but typically patients recover with no lasting effects. They wanted to continue monitoring Brooke for thirty-six more hours, which meant that she would be admitted to the pediatric ward the next day. He said we should try to get some rest tonight, and we'd talk more in the morning. We asked if he would pump her stomach or give her charcoal. He said those were not necessary for this situation.

Bryan left after that, and I returned to Brooke's room. She was sleeping, and I tried to get comfortable on the large armchair in the room. I could tell that it was made to recline and maybe even lay completely flat, but there didn't seem to be room for that in between Brooke's bed and the table against the wall. Instead of making noise rearranging the chair, I sat on it and leaned over, laying my head on the small bedside table with my arm underneath. I was basically folded in half all night.

As I tried to rest in this convoluted position, my mind raced with thoughts. I felt grateful that we found Brooke when we did, but I couldn't begin to answer the questions of why she did it or what comes next. How could I ever know she was safe in the future? How will this affect my other children? What will we say to our extended family? It was the first of many restless nights.

CHAPTER 8

Two Tense Days

Early Monday morning, Brooke and I were both awake, so I turned on the television. There wasn't much to watch, but at least it provided background noise. The ER nurse came in and asked Brooke how she felt and looked at her blood pressure, heart rate, and pulse oximeter numbers. A while later, the doctor came in. He said Brooke was stable, but her heart rate was still elevated. She would need to be admitted to the pediatric floor for another twenty-four hours of supervision. It took a few hours until they were ready for her, and there wasn't much to do in the small room.

Midmorning, a nurse escorted us up to the pediatric floor. The spacious room she took us to had a large window and a private bathroom. Brightly colored decorations and handmade drawings hung on the walls. The cheeriness was dampened, however, by the nurse's extensive and disheartening orientation to the room. I quickly realized they had a detailed protocol for patients who had attempted suicide. The nurse explained that Brooke could wear underwear, socks, and a hospital gown, but nothing else. She could ask for paper, pen, markers, or other supplies, but she could not have a backpack, bag, or any of her own items brought from home. The nurse would remain in the room at all times, and Brooke wasn't allowed to close the door to go to the bathroom. These rules reminded me of the gravity of our situation and the long road ahead of us.

Brooke seemed to be in moderate spirits, though. I wondered what she was thinking and feeling. Was she relieved or disappointed that her attempt wasn't successful? Was she nervous about the future? Did she have any effects from the overdose, such as foggy thinking or physical illness? Did she feel any regret, shame, or guilt? It was hard to tell. She didn't talk much. I asked occasionally how she was doing and if she needed anything. We talked about what she wanted to order from the cafeteria and what she wanted to watch on TV. She was kind and polite to the nurses but didn't converse much beyond the basics.

Bryan came back to the hospital around eleven a.m. He called me from the lobby, and I guided him to Brooke's new room. We were lucky they allowed both parents to be with Brooke, considering the Covid restrictions. When Bryan arrived, we requested a meeting with the crisis counselor. The nurse said he was with someone else but would be up to talk with us in about an hour.

Bryan and I went to a waiting room for patients' families to talk more freely and get caught up. The room was open and airy even though it lacked windows. There were multiple couches, a TV, and a small kitchen area supplied with snacks and drinks. This part of the hospital had been recently expanded and rebuilt, so the decorations and fixtures were modern and new. We had the room to ourselves, but we still closed the door for privacy. Bryan seemed worn out and distraught. We sat on the couch together and talked.

Bryan said when Sydney woke up that morning, he told her what had happened. He cried and she cried. He said that she didn't need to go to school that day. Kaitlin and Ben came and picked her up. Then Bryan talked to his brother Mike. Because they lived close to us, our kids went to school together. Bryan called to tell him Sydney wasn't going to school and explained why. After that, he had to go to work and explain the whole thing again. It was agonizing to relive the situation and go through the raw emotions again and again. Everyone at his office was kind and understanding. They rescheduled most of his patients, and he completed the one procedure that couldn't be delayed.

As we finished talking about Bryan's work, I received multiple texts from Kaitlin. I grabbed a granola bar from the counter and chewed it while I read. She said she had information about Brooke that she thought she should share. She sent screenshots of a recent text conversation between her and Brooke after one of our Sunday family dinners. Apparently, Bryan had said some things that bothered Brooke. The contents were both enlightening and distressing.

From Brooke:

bleh those conversations with dad are sometimes frustrating cuz i feel like he just doesn't understand how personal it is to me. like most of the points he makes are super true and it's a good reminder but he often makes me feel like i shouldn't feel extreme about these things when i probably should be less "im always right and this is the only side" about them but also it's a lot more personal to me than it is to him so of course im going to jump to more extremes and get angry. he says a lot of hurtful things about trans people.

that's just my mini rant.

also I've been thinking about this for a long time now and im definitely bisexual and like all genders and im most likely nonbinary, which might be a surprise. my closest friends have started using they/them pronouns for me and i really really love it, but i think id say my pronouns are they/she because i prefer they/them but im also OK with she/her. so yeah that's about where i am with that :)

which makes it also frustrating to talk about these things with dad cuz I'm not out to him about any of that stuff and so he doesn't know how personal the gay/trans rights are to me and i know he probably will never respect me being nonbinary if i come out to him.

I wasn't shocked or upset to learn of Brooke's identity. I nodded my head and thought, "Okay, this is something we will deal with." I wanted to read the rest of the conversation to get the whole picture.

In Kaitlin's response, she told Brooke that she also feels like these issues are more personal to her and that Bryan doesn't understand that. She thanked Brooke for sharing about her identity and emphasized that she loves and supports Brooke no matter what. She said, "I'm happy to hear that you've found something that feels right. Identity can be hard to figure out when you've been socialized to think you should be one way."

When Kaitlin was a freshman in college, she told us she was bisexual. I regret the way I handled it. The revelation was unexpected, and I was unprepared. I expressed doubts that she really knew because she hadn't had a lot of sexual experience. I asked her not to tell the other kids because it would confuse them. Shortly after that, she met Ben. When they got engaged later that year, Kaitlin's sexual identity came up again. When she talked about it, I said, "Is Ben okay with it? It seems like you might not want to stay with one person because you'll cut yourself off from that whole other experience." I see now that this was an offensive comment. Bisexual people are as able and likely to be faithful and have monogamous relationships as heterosexual people. The only difference is bisexual people pick the person they commit to from a choice of both genders instead of one.

Kaitlin referred to this situation as she encouraged Brooke to give us, her parents, a chance to be supportive. She said:

> ...you might be surprised with dad. I think at the least he would listen and respect you even if he

> doesn't fully understand... I think they're both open to learning though, even though it doesn't always feel like it. When I first went on medication for my depression and anxiety, they were super against it, which was hurtful to me because to me it was SUCH a relief to be on it and get some stability. But we talked a lot about it, and I shared how hurtful it was for them to have attitudes like that and they honestly changed their tune. Same with coming out as bi. Mom said some wild biphobic stuff out of ignorance and my instinct was just to deflect and hang up but actually talking to her and explaining my perspective resulted in a good conversation. None of that is to say that you have to say anything to them before you're ready or even ever, but just to say that you might be pleasantly surprised if you're prepared to have some vulnerable conversations.

I was thankful that Kaitlin was there for Brooke and gave Brooke such supportive and insightful advice. I realized that what I previously saw as a hardship (Kaitlin's bisexual identity) prepared me for the future.

In Brooke's next text, she thanked Kaitlin for her support and for sharing her experiences. She told Kaitlin that she'd been struggling with depression and anxiety, that she had told us, and that we'd helped her get therapy and medication. She said Kaitlin's willingness to have those hard conversations with us made it possible for her to get the help she needed. She agreed that Kaitlin had paved the way for her to come out to us. She felt that we may never understand trans people but maybe we could learn to respect them. After telling Kaitlin she loved her, she said, "It's been such a journey and it's still confusing, but nonbinary feels right and so do they/she pronouns. I love that I have you in my family who I can feel comfortable enough to tell this to and know you accept, understand, and love me. It seriously means the world."

Again, I felt comforted knowing that Brooke had someone on her side with whom she could discuss these difficult topics. Kaitlin and Brooke were the two children in our family who looked and acted the most alike. It was endearing that they were aligned on these issues and had similar identities also.

Their text conversation continued. They talked about how our family needs to do a better job of talking about uncomfortable subjects. They commented that we haven't been very open in the past and they would like to change that. This reminded me of some comments Haley had made recently. After spending the summer with Amanda's family in Georgia, she mentioned how unguarded the Thompsons were, how they talked about their mental health struggles and their medications. I felt defensive when she brought this up and wanted to point out that our family has other strengths that she doesn't notice or appreciate. But after reading the text trail between Kaitlin and Brooke about this same issue, I let my defenses drop and acknowledged that maybe we should work on that.

After I read the screenshotted texts, I sent a message to Kaitlin thanking her for sending them. She texted back that she didn't want to break Brooke's trust, but she felt that under these circumstances, it was warranted, and we needed to know about this conversation. Bryan had been working on his phone on the couch beside me while I read. When

I was done, I handed the phone to him to read the conversation. He was more shocked and shaken than I was. He obviously felt horrible that Brooke was hurt by what he had said and wished he could go back in time and redo those conversations. We knew we couldn't speak to Brooke about this directly right now, but we hoped that she would soon feel comfortable sharing her identity with us.

Those texts were hard to read, but what we had to do next was even more arduous. We needed to tell Haley. Haley's mission had rules about how and when you could communicate with family and friends. The president of the mission wanted the missionaries to be focused on the work of sharing the gospel and not be distracted by reminders of the parts of your life you had left behind for eighteen months. Therefore, we needed to talk to the president first to ask for permission to call Haley. We wanted to let him know about this situation anyway because it would affect Haley's wellbeing and productivity. I searched for an email from the mission about where to send Christmas packages. Luckily, I had saved it; at the bottom it had a phone number for the mission office. I went to the bathroom while Bryan called that number and spoke with the president.

When I got back, Bryan said the president was kind and sympathetic. He gave us permission to talk to Haley as much as we needed to this week. It was Monday, one of the days we had our regular scheduled phone calls with Haley. Our habit was to message in the morning to arrange a time. It was one in the afternoon by now, so I knew she would be wondering why we hadn't reached out. Bryan wasn't normally a part of the Monday conversations because they happened during the day when he was at work. We looked at each other and took a deep breath. We knew this would hit Haley hard, and we wished we could be there with her physically to support her after she heard the news. We hated to make the call, but we knew we had to.

We clicked the button to start a video chat. When Haley answered, she was still talking to a friend in her apartment and laughing with her. We said hello, she turned and focused on us, and then she became serious. She knew it was odd that we were both on the screen, and I'm sure she could tell from our faces that something was wrong. Electric pulses of nervousness went down my arms repeatedly. I wished that I did not have to say the words. I wished that I could tell her something else, something light and humorous. It felt like there was a rock in my throat, and tears ran down my face before I even spoke. This was one of the hardest things I've ever had to do. I was thankful for the privacy of the family waiting room.

"Haley, something has happened," I managed to say. She looked at us intensely and her eyes began to well with tears. "It's Brooke. She took some pills last night and we're in the hospital now. She's okay, but it was a serious attempt to take her own life." I sobbed in between phrases but got the words out. Haley started crying immediately. Her roommates came over and put their arms around her. We explained what we knew about her condition and her future treatment. It was excruciating to be so far from Haley and not be able to give her a hug and console her. I knew this would be hard for her to deal with, being away from the family and processing her emotions on her own. We tried to comfort her as best we could. We talked for a minute more and then said we'd call her again the next day.

That night I slept at the hospital. Bryan left before dinner, picked up Sydney, and they both slept at home. The counselor we'd spoken with during the night was off the next day. His replacement had been apprised of the situation and was working on finding an inpatient placement for Brooke. We received updates from him off and on throughout the day.

After talking with Haley, I had gone home to sleep for a few hours in the afternoon and to take a shower. It felt like I was in a trance the whole time. I slept restlessly; my eyes were stinging and sore from crying. I was thankful to be back at the hospital before too long, and I brought some stuff to stay overnight with Brooke. The room on the pediatric ward had a bigger armchair that reclined into a fully flat bed. It was more comfortable than the night before, but I still did not sleep well. Halfway through the night I realized that I could've brought pajamas or at least comfortable pants. As it was, I slept in my jeans, which gathered around the knees and hindered circulation to my lower legs.

I stayed in those jeans all the next day, Tuesday, mostly sitting in a chair next to Brooke's bed. We watched movies, she slept a lot, I worked on my computer. The nurses took Brooke's vitals at intervals, and the doctor came in to check on her occasionally. Brooke and I had a few short conversations. She seemed listless most of the day. When I asked how she was doing, she simply replied, "Okay." Sometimes she asked me to get her a blanket or order food for her. She didn't seem to want to talk much, but she did ask what was going to happen after she got released from the hospital. I told her the counselor was looking into places she could go and get more help. I told her these were like hospitals, but for mental health. She seemed encouraged by this idea. She asked throughout the day if we had heard anything more.

Bryan went to work that morning and joined me at the hospital after lunch. We reviewed what had happened to each of us since we'd last been together. His report was heartbreaking. He and Sydney had gotten fast food for dinner and then went home and watched TV together. Sydney went upstairs to get ready for bed but came back down shortly. She had tears in her eyes and said, "Dad, I should've known."

"What do you mean?" Bryan asked.

"I should've known that Brooke was going to do something. She cleaned her side of the bathroom, put everything away and wiped the counters. I noticed it Sunday night and thought that it was odd. She doesn't usually do that unless it's her day to clean the bathrooms. I should've known something was up and told you guys." She cried softly.

"Oh, honey, of course, you couldn't have known. Don't think that. None of us could have known. It's okay." He hugged her and consoled her and walked her up to her room. He saw the door to Brooke's room and tried not to think about the emptiness on the other side.

Sydney stayed home from school again on Tuesday. Kaitlin and Ben came to our house this time to be with her while Bryan was gone. Like the rest of the world, Kaitlin's university courses were completely online, as was Ben's job. It was convenient that they could be with Sydney and still accomplish what they needed to.

Bryan had a second highly unusual day of rearranging his schedule for a family emergency. In the morning, he saw the urgent cases. The rest were moved to a different day or another provider's schedule. More of his staff noticed this change, and he had more conversations about what had happened. I wasn't envious of his interactions with the outside world. He had to decide at each turn whether to evade the questions or explain what happened, neither of which was enjoyable.

During one of the doctor's visits to Brooke's room on Tuesday, he gave us an update on her condition. He reminded us that Brooke was admitted for observation of the symptoms of serotonin syndrome. He explained that she had never developed the more dangerous signs they watched for. Her heart rate was elevated for a time but was coming back down to normal now. He wanted to watch her for a few more hours, but he anticipated she would be released that day. That meant we needed to solidify a placement for her. I was terrified of the idea that we might have to bring her home. I knew that time in an inpatient behavioral health unit would help her get stabilized emotionally and start her on the pathway back to better mental health. Also, the professionals at that unit could guide us in how to take care of her when she did come home. We weren't sure what would happen to her after the inpatient stay. The counselor had mentioned some day treatment centers, but we hadn't had time to talk more about it or investigate those yet.

After speaking with the doctor, we requested another meeting with the counselor to see if there was a place for Brooke. He came promptly and we spoke out in the hall. The person we'd worked with the first night was back on duty. It was comforting to see him again. He said that he'd been on the phone with multiple centers. The only one with openings right now was in a city about an hour away from where we lived. It was a youth behavioral health unit inside a hospital. It had a good reputation, although he didn't know anyone personally who had been there. Bryan and I looked at each other. We knew we weren't ready to bring Brooke home, so we felt we had no other choice. We asked him to set it up.

The counselor came back in about an hour and said it was arranged. We could take Brooke there that night, when she was released from the hospital. He gave me a list of items Brooke could and couldn't bring. The instructions reminded me of the orientation to the hospital room on the pediatric floor: the patient is allowed few personal possessions and will be monitored at all times. We went back to Brooke's hospital room and talked to her about the placement. She seemed relieved to be going somewhere to get continued care, but she didn't have much to say beyond that. I asked her which pillow and blanket she wanted me to get and what clothes to pack.

Bryan stayed at the hospital while I went back to the house. I sat with Kaitlin, Ben, and Sydney for a while, asking how they were feeling and what they had been doing. I thanked Kaitlin and Ben for staying there and helping us out. Everyone was somber. I told them that Brooke was going to an inpatient unit for a few days; we weren't sure how long she'd be there.

I gathered the items Brooke would need and packed them in a duffle bag. It was dark as I drove back to the hospital. The roads seemed empty and quiet. I didn't listen to my usual podcasts or audiobooks in the car but drove in silence. Once

I returned, Bryan and I got Brooke checked out of the hospital and loaded into the car. The hour-long drive to the next hospital was also hushed. Bryan drove; I sat in the back with Brooke, which felt odd, but I wanted to monitor how she was doing. We let Brooke have her phone for part of the drive. She typed and read texts the whole time. When I asked what she was doing, she said letting her friends know where she was going. I wished I could read those texts. I wished I knew what was going on in her head. Was she ashamed, sorrowful, empty, raging? The counselor had told us that many teenagers resist going to inpatient units. They get angry and defiant. Brooke, however, was her usual compliant, acquiescent self. She didn't question why she had to go or complain about it. Maybe that meant she felt it would help her. Hopefully she wanted to be helped. That would make her treatment more effective.

We were in and out of the new hospital in about an hour; most of that time was spent waiting. Bryan, Brooke, and I donned our masks once again as we entered and checked in at the emergency room. Eventually, someone from the behavioral health unit came to get us. They took us to the fourth floor and said only one parent could come in with Brooke because of Covid restrictions. Bryan stayed in the lobby, and I went in through the locked doors with Brooke, where we waited again. Finally, a nurse came and spoke with us. She entered our intake data into the computer and then gave me paperwork that explained the policies and procedures of the unit. She said that the next day they would do a full set of evaluations to determine how long Brooke would need to stay. The usual length of stay was about five days, so at least I had a reference point. Visiting hours were limited because of Covid, but because we lived over an hour away, it would be difficult for us to visit anyway. Luckily, they allowed the patients to video chat with their families during certain times of the day.

Brooke was quiet and tense beside me, but she answered questions the nurse directed to her. After the intake, we walked together to her assigned room. The unit seemed new and well-run. There was a gathering area with a TV, games, and craft supplies. The nurse explained that Brooke's day would be filled with individual and group therapy as well as enrichment activities. Brooke's room was spacious and had a large window. The blinds to the window were in between two panes of glass. The furniture was minimal, of course. A simple desk and chair, some shelves and drawers, and an austere-looking bed attached to the wall and overlaid with one blanket. The nurse left us alone in the room to say goodbye. We unpacked Brooke's stuff and chatted a little.

I didn't know how I was supposed to feel. I thought that many parents would be overwhelmed or distraught. But I felt my usual peculiar calm. I thought I should be more upset to leave her there. I wondered if she thought I was too unemotional. My instinct, however, was to do what needed to be done, keep taking the next step forward. I was sorrowful that this was happening and worried about her distress, but it seemed illogical and unnecessary to make a big emotional show of it. The whole thing felt surreal. Just have a hug, say goodbye and I love you, walk out the door and back to the car. Keep going.

I gave Bryan the recap on the drive home. I told him the staff looked friendly and capable, and the place seemed professional. The rules were reasonable, and the therapists and aides appeared eager to help the patients. I said Brooke was quiet but apprehensive. We both hoped that she would feel comfortable there and get used to it quickly. I told him that I would have video calls with her daily, and I would come up in two days to visit her in person. We both felt a sense of relief, appreciative that someone else would oversee her health and safety for a while. For the first time in forty-eight hours, we felt tentatively reassured. Hopefully, this inpatient unit would help Brooke get better and help us know how to take care of her.

CHAPTER 9

Operation Time Go By

Thursday morning, two days after we dropped Brooke off at the behavioral health unit, I found myself at the doctor's office. The previous night my left calf had started to ache and swell. It was stiff and felt hard when pressed. Bryan worried it was a deep vein thrombosis or DVT, a clot that develops in the calf after sitting for long periods of time. The clot can get loose, travel up to the lungs, and cause a serious obstruction in one of the pulmonary arteries.

When my calf started hurting, I recalled that I had sat in the chair next to Brooke's hospital bed for most of the previous day, rarely getting up to stretch or take a walk. I'm sure the jeans tight around my knees didn't help either. Luckily, Bryan made some calls, and I was able to be seen that morning. The ultrasound technician scanned my leg from midcalf to where the vein reaches the groin area. When he finished, he called Bryan and said it was nothing serious. There was a clot in the calf, but it was in a more superficial vein and could not travel to the lungs. He recommended heat, elevation, and rest to reduce the aching and swelling.

I was relieved to hear that I wasn't in danger. I stopped for fast food after the appointment and ate on my drive up to see Brooke. To make it in time for visiting hours, I needed to hurry. As I drove, I mentally reviewed the events of the previous day. It had felt luxurious to sleep in my own bed again after two nights in the hospital, even though my continued worry about Brooke prevented a perfectly restful sleep. I didn't have anything scheduled on Wednesday and took a nap later in the day, between my Brooke-related tasks. Bryan went back to a regular day of work, and Sydney went back to school.

I spent much of Wednesday researching treatment options on the internet and by phone. I thought that after Brooke's inpatient stay, she would start intensive outpatient, or IOP. This is a transition period between inpatient hospitalization and readmission to the real world. Patients live at home but have individual and group therapy multiple times a week to get support and build coping skills. But the counselor at the hospital had told us that the model had changed. IOP wasn't a common option, but there was a program called day treatment. This was often held at residential treatment centers, but the day treatment patients went home each night instead of staying at the center. There were a few of these scattered throughout our region. The counselor had pointed one or two out that had bad reputations, but otherwise he didn't give much direction.

It can be difficult to navigate this system and know which places are helpful and which have problems. However, a friend of mine put me in touch with one of her friends, Nancy, whose child had recently spent time in a day treatment center, and she was able to guide me. Nancy had experience with some of the inpatient behavioral health units in our region, also. There was another inpatient facility closer to our home that we had hoped to get Brooke into, but Nancy told me her son had been there, and it wasn't that great. That made me feel better about having to send Brooke so far away. She said her son's time in the program was beneficial. He attended all day, eight a.m. to five p.m., for about six weeks. They had him do schoolwork there as well as individual and group therapy. This seemed like an ideal situation. Professionals would watch over Brooke and guide her psychological care and her schooling, but she would get to come home each night to be with us. I had heard about some troubles with residential treatment centers and would be nervous to send Brooke there and not see her every day.

Midmorning on Wednesday, I sat at my desk in the office and started a Google search for day treatment centers. A few came up, but not all the ones I had heard of. It took more digging to find addresses and numbers for those. I made a list in a notebook and took notes on the different places. Some were close by, some further away; some took our insurance, some didn't; some I had heard of (good and bad) and some I hadn't. I called many places and left a lot of messages. When I was able to speak to someone, most of them said they didn't have any spots. Some said I could fill out the application, and they would consider Brooke when and if a spot opened. They could not say how long that would be. The applications were lengthy and time consuming.

The last several days had been some of the most difficult in my life, and now I faced the challenging task of finding an adequate placement for Brooke after her inpatient stay. Everyone agreed she needed additional care, but space issues and the rising number of teens in mental health crisis made me worry about finding a spot for her. I was nervous about having her home under my and Bryan's supervision, concerned that we wouldn't know the right things to do to keep her safe.

It was a stressful process on many levels. I didn't know how to pick the right place. Each center had many positive reviews, but there were always a small number of negative ones accusing the staff of harm or neglect and the doctors of indifference. It was hard to know who to trust. The place my nephew had attended was not close to us and would require a lot of driving to get Brooke there and back every day. But my brother had highly recommended it, so it might be worth it. When I called that facility, however, they said they do not take our insurance plan.

Another nerve-wracking aspect was the timing. I had to put Brooke's name on multiple waiting lists and hope something worked out. We didn't know when she would come home from the behavioral health unit (that was part of the problem), and the centers didn't know when they'd have space. It seemed like a miracle would have to occur for it to work out. I desperately wanted Brooke to have a place to go. I knew she wasn't emotionally equipped to go back to high school, and

I felt unqualified to monitor her all day if she stayed home. I needed her to get into one of these places, and if it could be an amazing place, that would be a bonus.

At three p.m., I took a break from the research and called the hospital where Brooke was staying. The online visiting hours were between three and four p.m. I requested to talk to Brooke, and she called me back with a video chat. Our conversation had an odd quality to it, not surprisingly, but Brooke seemed to be doing well. She told me about people she had met and the activities they had done. She said it was hard to sleep on the uncomfortable bed, but that the staff were nice and friendly. I wasn't sure what to say. I didn't want to ask, "Are you feeling better? All healed?" because I knew that improvement in mental health takes time, and I didn't want to pressure her into saying yes or pretending to be better than she was.

As I got closer to the hospital to visit Brooke, my reminiscing about the day before changed to wondering how she would be today. Maybe she would be bored of the place and ask to go home, maybe mad at someone there and need to vent. I hoped that I could be what she needed me to, be sympathetic to her but also encourage her to get better. One last thing my mind reviewed before I got there was my conversation with Haley the previous day. She was anxious to know what was happening with Brooke. I messaged her first to find a good time to talk. When she was ready, I called her and gave her the update on Brooke. She was relieved to hear that we'd found a good inpatient placement for her and wanted to know more about the day treatment options. I tried to reassure her that everything would be okay, but she seemed down and anxious. She again expressed her wish that she could be closer to us.

I drove up to the hospital and found the parking lot. I had been to this area before, but the hospital had been remodeled since I'd last seen it. It was a large, beautiful building with lots of windows and tan and gray brick. I walked in and was unnerved by the emptiness of the lobby until I remembered the Covid restrictions. Someone monitored visitors to make sure they had a legitimate reason to be there and that they wore a mask. I told the woman I was there to visit my daughter, and she let me through. I went up the elevator to the fourth floor, found the behavioral health unit, and pushed the button to alert them I was waiting. An employee came and opened the door. She said to leave my purse in the cubbies in the ante room, and she scanned my body for any metal objects I might be concealing. Finally, she opened the main door to the unit and walked me to Brooke's room.

"Hi, Mom!" Brooke seemed cheery and at ease. She wore sweats and a t-shirt and sat on her bed. I saw half-filled coloring pages and crayons on the desk. Sunbeams shone through the window.

"How are you doing?" I had that awkward, not-sure-how-to-be feeling, but I wanted to act normal for Brooke.

"Pretty good," she replied.

"What have you been doing?"

She told me about the various activities and therapy sessions. She was talkative and even jovial. I asked questions in between, and she was happy to answer them. She told me about the others in her groups. Many of them had been in multiple inpatient and residential treatment programs, so she was learning a lot about "the system." Some of the friends she had made told her about difficult home situations. I hoped this would help Brooke realize the positive aspects of her life. A nurse came by during our discussion and gave Brooke her medicine. With our consent, they had put Brooke on Zoloft, which seemed like a more standard antidepressant. They also prescribed propranolol, a betablocker that reduces the anxiety response in the body without any mind-altering effects.

Brooke talked a lot about the food, what she ordered for each meal and how good or not good it tasted. I gave her updates from home, about Sydney's classes and Bryan's work. Brooke said she liked her therapist and told me about the concepts she'd learned. It sounded positive and helpful. The time went by quickly and eventually the nurse came in and said visiting hours were about over. Brooke seemed ready to be on her own again, which comforted me. But still, it was bizarre to give her a hug, say goodbye, and leave her there, not for a medical condition but for psychiatric care. It didn't seem real.

I spoke with a nurse on the way out about the time frame for Brooke's release. She said she thought it would be Sunday, but the doctor would call me that day or the next to let me know for sure. After going down the elevator, I sat in the hospital lobby for a while before driving home. I had to make follow-up calls with various day treatment centers before the workday was over. I had received a few voicemails and emails that were encouraging. It was awkward timing though because the next week was Thanksgiving. The various centers were either closed or weren't taking new patients for all or part of that week. I wanted to get as much done as I could this week so there wouldn't be any more delay than necessary. It was starting to look like Brooke would spend Thanksgiving week at home with us. Hopefully, by the Monday after Thanksgiving there would be a spot for her. It made me nervous to think about having her at home full time. On the drive home, I made plans in my head to keep her occupied and always supervised.

I woke up Friday morning knowing I had a difficult task ahead. It was time to call my parents and tell them what had happened. First, I exercised and got ready for the day, then I sat down in my office chair. I looked out the window onto our front lawn and contemplated the calls. Our street still had houses under construction. Dumpsters, large trucks, and other construction equipment were scattered along the road. The sounds of trucks rumbling down the street, hammers pounding, and the beeping signals of vehicles in reverse were not uncommon. I brought my attention back to the room, picked up my phone, and opened it. It had taken me this long to feel ready to talk about what had happened. Bryan had told his brother, people at his work, and a few people from church with whom he regularly interacted, but I had not told anyone except my brother (only because I needed his advice). However, I didn't feel I should put it off any longer.

My parents are divorced, so this required two separate calls. It was basically the same conversation with both. I cried when I told them the story. They were shocked but kind and sympathetic. They asked questions about where she was now and where she would go next. They offered to help any way they could. My dad expressed confusion. He said, "She always seems so happy to me." This seemed irrelevant because of course she put on a happy face when she was around others, that's what most people do. He doesn't see her often, and when he does, it's for short periods of time. Still, he couldn't seem to grasp that she had an invisible internal struggle going on. He would voice this bewilderment many times in the coming months.

My parents, like many of their generation, are mystified by emotional struggles like anxiety and depression. My mom seems to have more serotonin than my whole family combined, a fact that I have been envious of throughout the years. She wears rose-colored glasses and favors hyperbole. When she tells a story, it's always the most amazing food, the most beautiful decorations, the most talented people with whom she interacts. She tells me often how wonderful I am and how thankful she is that we're so close, even as I feel guilty for being grumpy while we're together. She tries to be supportive of our family's struggles with mental health, but I know she doesn't really understand them.

One reason my parents had trouble staying together was that my mom is quite social, and my dad is not. He is content to stay in his office for hours at a time, working on bills or taxes (he is an accountant), unaware of other members of the family. However, he is caring and thoughtful. He never forgets a birthday or holiday and makes a lot of effort to spend time with me and my family. He is also pragmatic and logical. He asks a lot of questions, and he likes things planned out in advance. He doesn't experience a lot of emotional highs and lows and has difficulty relating to those who do.

I felt relief when those calls were over, even though my eyes were stinging and throbbing from crying. My next task was to find Brooke a new therapist. After she told me a few weeks ago that she didn't like Sarah, she tried a man named Shawn, also over Zoom. It only took one session for her to veto him. Then I found a place prosaically named The Counseling Clinic. The two main counselors did not have openings, but they had an intern named Bridget who could see Brooke—and the sessions were in person! This made a big difference to Brooke, and she liked Bridget a lot.

However, the previous Saturday (the day before Brooke's suicide attempt), I had received an email from Lynn, Bridget's supervisor, and the owner of The Counseling Clinic. She said that for personal reasons, Bridget was leaving the clinic for a time. I had told Brooke the news that night and said we'd have to look for another one. Now I wondered if that was somehow a final moment for Brooke in her despair. She'd been through so many counselors, it had to be discouraging that when she had found someone she connected with, that person left.

I emailed Lynn and explained why I hadn't replied since Saturday. I told her what had happened and where Brooke was now. I said Brooke would likely be in day treatment for six to eight weeks, and I asked her if she had time to see Brooke as a client after that. Within minutes of sending the email, I had a response from Lynn. She expressed her sympathy for our situation and said that she could take Brooke after she completed the day treatment program.

By this time, two centers had sent emails saying it looked like they would have room for Brooke after the week of Thanksgiving. All the others seemed like dead ends. They either hadn't replied to my messages or said they were full and wouldn't have space any time soon. To move ahead with the two centers with openings, I had to fill out their extensive online applications. Besides demographic information, they had forms assessing Brooke's current mental state, as well as our family dynamics. They wanted insurance information, HIPPA signatures, pharmacy preferences, and lists of previous physicians. Although this process took time and emotional energy, I felt fortunate because we had an insurance plan with generous coverage, and I had the time, resources, and knowledge to navigate the system. I spent the rest of the afternoon working on the applications, with a short break to video chat with Brooke.

Sunday afternoon I drove again to the hospital where Brooke was staying and picked her up. The doctor had called me on Saturday and apprised me of Brooke's progress and current state. He said he felt comfortable sending her home, and he was happy to hear that we had some leads on day treatment centers. He said he had enjoyed getting to know and working with Brooke. This is what everyone who interacts with Brooke says. She is such a joy to be with, so bright and interesting and easy to talk to, even when she is in an inpatient behavioral health unit. The doctor expressed optimism for Brooke's future, which was great to hear. He explained more about the medications they had prescribed for her and said we would need to see a local doctor to continue the prescriptions.

When I saw Brooke, after I had deposited my things in the cubbies, passed the metal detector, and was let in through the locked doors, she seemed eager to go.

"How come you didn't come earlier?" she questioned me. It was true that I could have come earlier in the day, but frankly,

I was nervous to come get her. I wanted to put off bringing her home for a few more hours. Home—when she was last there, she thought things were so awful that she should end her life. I did not relish the idea of bringing her back there.

On the drive back, the sky was gray and cloudy. The mountains to the east were mostly brown, but still showed patches of orange or red from the fall colors of the trees. I told Brooke about what I called Operation Time Go By. I explained that the medications can take weeks to have effect, and so we needed to simply have time pass. She doesn't have to accomplish anything; she doesn't have to go to school. We wanted life to be easy for her. But that didn't mean sitting around. I had plans and a schedule. I wanted her to get plenty of sleep, walk every day, meditate, read self-help books, make gratitude lists, and repeat affirmations. I had a list of everything that has ever shown efficacy in improving mood and a time schedule for how to do them all in a day. I tried to present this plan breezily and without too much pressure. Brooke didn't like the idea of a set schedule, but she agreed to do most of the tasks if she could choose the order.

When we got home on Sunday, Kaitlin and Ben were there for Sunday dinner. The meal and conversation were as normal as could be expected, under the circumstances. We called Haley on a video chat so she and Brooke could talk. During that week, I didn't leave the house without having Brooke with me or knowing where she was. I checked in with her frequently. Gwen was home for Thanksgiving, so Brooke spent a lot of time with her. That relieved me on many levels: Brooke enjoys being with Gwen, I got a break from supervising duties, and social interactions are mood-boosting in general.

We hosted Thanksgiving dinner at our house. Bryan's family had planned to come, but because the Covid numbers were rising, most of them decided to stay home. Mike and Josie and their kids came over. We saw them so often we considered them part of our "bubble." And my dad came down for dinner. Mike and Josie brought a lot of the food. It was a casual meal, and everyone was comfortable, all things considered.

On Friday, we got confirmation that Brooke could attend a day treatment center called Brighter Days. It was a forty-minute drive, but it seemed like a good option, and it was the only one with an open spot. Thankfully, I didn't have any work commitments at the time and could drive Brooke there and back every day. And they accepted our insurance. We had already met our deductible, so we would only be responsible for a twenty percent copay. We rested easier knowing there was a plan in place.

Sometime during that week, Bryan and I revisited the topic of Brooke's hair and piercings. We saw our rigid rules in a whole new light. We regretted forcing Brooke to stick to our standards, standards she did not believe in or agree with. We obviously wanted to do whatever we could to make Brooke feel comfortable at home and accepted by us. We also wanted her to know undoubtedly that we would love her no matter what. We discussed how to approach this and decided together what to say. One afternoon I found Brooke downstairs on the couch watching TV and had a talk with her.

"Dad and I have been talking, and we want to apologize for having such strict rules about hair dye and piercings," I started. Brooke had an apprehensive look, like she was wondering where this was going. The basement was cool; Brooke had a blanket around her legs. There was a fireplace in the corner, but it was not on.

I continued, "We want you to know that we love you no matter what. We fear it might have come across as if you must follow the church standards and rules for us to love and accept you. So, we want to tell you that you are more important to us than the church or the church standards. Whatever you do or whoever you are, we will always love you. If you drink or smoke, swear or commit crimes, if you are gay or bisexual, and however you want to look, we will accept and care for you. You are always welcome here. We have realized that this may not have been the message you've received. It might have felt like our love was conditional, but it's not."

Brooke still didn't show much emotion, but hopefully the message was sinking in. Maybe it was hard for her to believe we were sincere after years of rules and lessons about how she should look and act. I wanted to include the gay or bisexual part so she would feel more comfortable coming out to us and know that we would support her.

"Does that mean I can dye my hair again?" Brooke asked with medium excitement. Most of the color had faded from her hair, and she was ready for a color boost.

"Yes, you can dye it pink again, with an at-home dye." This was a surprise to her because in the past I was against at-home dying. I thought it didn't look as nice, but I gave up this preference along with so many others. I also told Brooke, "Maybe toward your birthday we can revisit more piercings, too." She seemed happy about this. I knew Bryan and I had work to do to get used to her new look and truly accept her, however she presented herself. But I was ready to do the work. I was ready to shed the constraints the church put on our behavior, the "shoulds," and the judgment of others. It felt freeing to let that go, even though I knew it would take time to get out of those habits.

CHAPTER 10

No Empty Chairs

One thing standing between Brooke and her day treatment center, Brighter Days, was a Covid test. She had to have a negative test within twenty-four hours before her first day. We wanted her to start on a Monday, but we couldn't find a testing site open on Sunday. We spoke with the center, and they instructed us to get the test on Monday and have Brooke come on Tuesday. Monday morning, I took her to get the test but found out an hour later that it was the wrong kind of test and wouldn't be back in time anyway. When Bryan got home from work that day, he drove her to a testing site a half hour away that had the correct type of test and could get us the results in an hour. Luckily, she tested negative and would be able to go to Brighter Days the next day.

During the forty-minute drive there on Tuesday, I could tell Brooke was nervous. The weather was still mild, and no snow had fallen yet. It was December 1st, a time that should be festive with the anticipation of Christmas. But the mood in the car was somber and somewhat foreboding. Brooke fidgeted with her clothes and her phone. She didn't look at me and gave short answers when I asked questions. I agonized for her. It must be intimidating to go to a new place where you don't know anyone or any of the routines. I wondered if she regretted taking the pills because it led to this, or maybe she wished they had done what she'd intended. She couldn't bring her phone into the day treatment, but she used it in the car. She texted and scrolled through Instagram at a frantic pace, her hands shaking slightly.

We got to the center at eight a.m., as they had instructed. I had done the paperwork I needed to, but I dropped Brooke off at the office so she could fill out more forms. When she was done, the receptionist would take her to the day treatment room. I was not allowed inside the building because of Covid restrictions, but the receptionist came out to greet me. We had spoken on the phone many times in the last few days as I tried to secure Brooke's placement. It was nice to put a face to the voice I was familiar with. After chatting with her, I turned to Brooke, gave her a hug, and said, "I love you" and "goodbye." She is such a cooperative child; she hadn't complained about coming to this program, even though she clearly was unsure about it. I felt so much love for her as I held her briefly. I was proud of her bravery to face this next challenge. I knew it was the right thing to do, but I felt unkind driving away and leaving her there.

It ended up being a difficult and volatile week. Brooke didn't say much about her time at the center the first few days. She went straight to her room when she got home and only came out to eat dinner with us. I could tell she was suffering, but I wasn't sure what to do. I knew it would get better with time. She did tell us that there were only six kids in the program with her. We were surprised about that, but, of course, we didn't know what to expect. She also said she didn't like any of the staff, which was disappointing.

On the drive to the center Thursday morning, I noticed cuts on the inside of Brooke's lower right arm. My stomach felt heavy and sick, but instead of feeling a rise in emotion, I felt a dip. The familiar, yet unnatural, stillness came over me. *We will deal with this. It will be okay.* We hadn't talked about self-harm since Brooke's first admission of depression and our conversation at the high school. Maybe she had discussed it with her therapists, but I hadn't brought it up. Part of me had forgotten about it, and part of me didn't want to bring it up.

However, I was less outraged or bewildered by self-harm behavior than a lot of parents might have been because I had learned about it in my social work training. Although I didn't have that desire, I understood that it can be a relief for people in severe emotional pain. It is fascinating that the same idea comes to many different people as a method of dealing with their sorrow. Even before social media, where youth could learn about these behaviors, some percentage of people suffering emotionally look at a knife or blade and have the same thought: running that across my skin will make me feel better. They experience that act differently than those not in emotional turmoil.

My mind reviewed this after I saw the wounds on Brooke's arm. I was thankful for my understanding of the issues and for my ability to stay calm and deliberate in my response instead of reacting adversely and without forethought. I thought about what Brooke had been through and wondered if this was a legitimate way of coping with the stress. A few months ago, I wouldn't have entertained that notion, but now I thought, if this is what she needs to do to deal with life but stay here with us, maybe it's okay.

We were nearing the center and the time to say goodbye. I wanted to mention the cuts, but I didn't know what to say. When we pulled up to the door, I put the car in park and faced Brooke.

"I see the cuts on your arm. When did you do that?" Inside, I asked the universe to help me say the right things.

Brooke glanced at me and then looked at her arm. "Last night."

"You must have been upset. I'm sorry that you're struggling." I wanted to begin with empathy before getting into the right or wrong of the behavior. I wasn't sure where I stood on the morality of it, anyway.

"It's okay." Brooke looked out the window, and I saw tears in her eyes. My heart melted. I wanted to reach over and do something that would make her pain go away.

I said, "I know this sometimes helps people feel better, but I'm still worried about it."

"I know." Brooke still faced the window.

"Let's talk about it more tonight." I didn't know what else to say. I leaned over to hug her and said goodbye.

I felt terrible on the drive home as my mind ran over and over the conversation. Halfway home I had a realization that gave me a glimmer of hope: Jill, the therapist assigned to Brooke at Brighter Days, had emailed me the day before to introduce herself. I could ask her for advice on what to do. As soon as I got home, I sat down at my computer and sent her an email. I explained what I had seen and that I didn't want to overreact or drive Brooke away. I wanted Brooke to be safe, of course, but also to feel comfortable talking to me about this in the future. Jill replied before long and proved to be a helpful resource. She complimented me on staying calm and gave suggestions for how to talk to Brooke.

That evening, I went up to Brooke's room. She was lying on her bed, scrolling through her phone. The blinds on her window were halfway open, but all I could see outside was darkness. I started off by saying that I was again sorry that she was going through this hard time. I asked what she thought of day treatment so far.

"I don't like it," Brooke responded. She said that the other kids were weird, and the staff weren't that great. She felt nervous every time she went. I asked if that's why she had cut on her arm. She nodded. I asked her to show me what she used to cut. She seemed annoyed and said, "Just a blade."

"What blade? Where did it come from?" I pressed. She said it was from a pencil sharpener; she had broken it apart and gotten the blade out. I asked her gently to show it to me. She was reluctant, but she finally got off the bed and walked into the bathroom. She found the small blade and showed me.

I said, "Like we talked about this morning, I don't blame you for trying something that you thought would help you feel better. I know you are doing your best. But I would like you to find other coping skills that aren't harmful to you. Do you think that'd be good?" She nodded. I went on, "I think that the therapists at day treatment will help you learn productive coping skills. I know you don't like it right now, but it will get better. You'll get used to it, and hopefully you'll feel better over time. Are you willing to keep trying?" She nodded again.

"I'd like you to give me the blade," I said gently. Jill had suggested that I ask to see the implement and ask for Brooke to give it to me. She said if she refused, that I could create a consequence. A common one is removing the door from a teenager's room. This is not physically harmful to them, but they don't like it. Teenagers value their privacy. As parents we want them to have that, but we need a way of motivating behavior that we know will be best in the long run. I hoped it wouldn't come to that, however, because I didn't know if I had the nerve to remove the door.

Luckily, Brooke slowly handed me the blade. I thanked her and hugged her. I told her again that it's going to be okay; things will get better. I asked her if there was anything I could do for her, but she said no. I knew it would be easy for Brooke to find another tool to use for self-harm, but I hoped that talking to her about it and asking her not to would make a difference, at least give her pause when she went to do it again. Maybe giving the blade to me would invoke some symbolism for stopping the behavior.

I realized that we needed to talk with Brooke on a regular basis about how she felt. I discussed this with Jill in my next email and asked for her advice. I wanted to query Brooke about her mental health, but I didn't want to annoy her by doing it too often. Jill and I agreed that three times a week was a good place to start. I like to have a system; I don't want to rely on my memory to occasionally ask. To that end, I put reminders in my phone for Sunday, Tuesday, and Thursday night. We told Brooke that we wanted to check on her wellbeing a few times a week and that we had four questions: How is your depression? How is your anxiety? What is your desire to self-harm? (This included cutting or taking pills or any other form of injury to self.) And finally, are you committed to getting better? This last question was Jill's suggestion and I liked it. It gave us a sense of Brooke's motivation, and it reminded her that it would take work to get better but that she could do it.

I was not used to talking openly with my children about hurting themselves. It felt awkward at first, but I knew it was the right thing to do. Speaking honestly about this not only allowed us to monitor Brooke's journey, but it also normalized talking about our struggles. It helped Brooke open up about other things, such as her frustrations with people at day treatment and her anxieties about getting better. We wanted to give the message that it's okay to feel that desire to self-harm, it's okay to talk about feeling that, and it's okay to ask for help when you feel like that or have any other problem. She seemed to understand that and to feel more comfortable talking to us. We decided to use a 1–10 scale for depression and anxiety (10 being the worst), a 1–5 scale for desire to self-harm, and a yes–no answer for the are-you-committed question. This became our habit, and soon enough we became comfortable discussing these issues.

The next few weeks went along smoothly. Brooke got familiar with the people and activities at Brighter Days. I got used to driving there and back twice a day. I didn't mind the long drive because it gave me a chance to be with Brooke in an easy setting. I made a rule that Brooke had to talk to me for ten minutes before getting on her phone. She was compliant with this rule, as usual. She softened and told me more stories about her day and her relationships at day treatment. We had at least ten minutes of fun conversations each day, and sometimes we talked through the whole drive. On the way home, alone in the car, I made phone calls or listened to podcasts or audiobooks.

One morning during our ten-minute talk time, I asked Brooke if she and Sam ever argue. Their relationship had continued to progress, despite the interruption of Brooke's time in the behavioral health unit. They had hung out over Thanksgiving break, and although she insisted that they were just friends, they texted or talked almost every day. However, I had looked in Brooke's sketch pad/journal again the week before and saw something I wanted to ask about. She had written another entry about a boy saying mean things about her to others. I couldn't get the context, so I thought I would explore it with Brooke, without letting her know what I had read. I didn't think the entry was about Sam, but I thought it didn't hurt to ask.

Brooke said no, she and Sam didn't argue. She asked me why I asked, and I said I was simply wondering. I asked if she fought with any other boys, currently or in the past, and she said no. This made me wonder about the writings in the notebook—were they real events or stories? I wanted to keep the conversation going, so I asked her if there were any boys she was interested in, besides possibly Sam. She said not really. The conversation fizzled after that.

That night as I was falling asleep, I realized this was the perfect opportunity to allow Brooke to talk about her sexual identity. At our family dinner the past Sunday, I had heard Kaitlin use the word "heteronormative." I'd never heard the word before, but I knew immediately what it meant: in your assumptions or questions, acting as if heterosexuality was the norm and failing to consider homosexual or other sexual identity options.

The next morning as we waited for the light leading out of our neighborhood to turn green, I said, "You know how yesterday I asked if there were any boys you were interested in? Well, I realized I was being heteronormative." I looked over at her with a little smile as I said the new word. "So, I wanted to also ask, are there any girls you are interested in?"

She looked surprised but smiled. She said, "No, not right now." She glanced at me again and said, "But I am bisexual." There it was, finally out in the open. I kept my face calm as I said, "You are?" She nodded and continued, "Also, I identify as non-binary."

My eyebrows raised. "Oh, really?" I questioned. "How long have you known that?"

"For a while now," she replied. "I wasn't sure if I wanted to tell you guys or what you would think."

Here was a pivotal moment, the time for a parent to say the right thing, create a bonding moment instead of a crisis or wedge in the relationship. I didn't know exactly how to respond, but I hoped I was up to the challenge.

"I'm glad you told me. That must have been hard to keep from us, knowing you felt like that. I'm sorry if that was hard for you. Are you okay if I tell dad?" I asked her as a courtesy, but I knew I would tell him regardless of what she said. I could not keep this from Bryan; we always talked things over and made decisions together.

I could tell Brooke was hesitant. "Yeah, I guess. I don't think he'll understand. He doesn't seem too supportive of LGBTQ identities."

"I think you underestimate him," I said. "He wants to do what's right for you and our family. He's willing to learn and ready to change. He loves you and wants to be a good father. Give him a chance, you'll see."

She looked relieved. I was glad to stick up for Bryan. If he had known what Brooke was going through, he never would have said those things about transgender or nonbinary people. He thought he was discussing the issues in an impersonal way, like any other current event. I knew he was prepared to open his mind to new ideas and become more accepting.

"What pronouns do you like to use?" I questioned. She said she liked they/them, but she knew it was hard to change and didn't feel that strongly about it. I sensed she downplayed her preferences and thought again about how she tends to acquiesce to the family to maintain pleasant feelings. I loved this about Brooke, but it possibly had a downside too. Maybe she was too eager to please; maybe she modulated her responses too much to make others happy.

I had one further question for Brooke. I thought I knew the answer already, but I wanted to discuss it openly with her. I said, "In light of this new information, how do you feel about the church?"

Our church is not very friendly toward or accepting of LGBTQ people. On the surface, church leaders will say we love all of God's children and we accept all people into our church regardless of race, gender, or sexual orientation. However, they will not hesitate to add that the doctrine of the church states that marriage between a man and a woman is the only type of marriage ordained by God, that there are only two genders, and that, as mortals, we cannot change God's laws. The highest leaders of our church have spoken about this more frequently as the world has become more accepting of these identities. Our church lobbied fervently against gay marriage before it became legal and encouraged members to do the same. If church members do come out as gay, they are encouraged to marry the opposite gender anyway or stay celibate to keep God's law of chastity. To families of our religion, having an LGBTQ child is upsetting and seen as a trial to work through.

Brooke shifted in her seat, glanced at me, and looked away. "I don't like going to church," she said slowly. I asked how long she had felt like this. "A few years," she responded. Just as I had suspected. She had always participated in church activities and done what we asked of her (said prayers, gone to youth summer camp, gave lessons or talks in church), but I often felt that her heart wasn't in it. It's hard to tell with teenagers, but something about Brooke had told me she didn't believe like we did. Now I had confirmation.

"It's okay," I told her. "I'm okay with you not being involved in the church." She didn't act visibly surprised, but this was probably not what she expected me to say. I asked her if she wanted to stop going.

"Well, I don't mind going. I know it's important to you guys, so if you want me to, I'll keep going with the family. But I don't believe any of the stuff." My heart melted hearing this response. Brooke is so sweet, always wanting to please us. I had a stab of guilt thinking about what we had asked of her in the past and all she did even though she didn't want to.

Many parents in our faith community would be distressed by this conversation, particularly the lack of interest in church. They would worry about their child following the precepts of the gospel and qualifying for heaven, and they would worry about the cohesiveness of their eternal family. "What if everyone else in the family made it to heaven, but this one child wasn't there with us?" they might ask themselves. That would be tragic. I've heard a saying from members of our church: "No empty chairs in heaven." Each person has a seat at the table, and if one of them doesn't make it to heaven, there will be an empty chair, and the rest of the family members will be forlorn.

Bryan and I have both felt for years that this was a manipulative and fear-based concept. It implies that everyone must be the same and take the same path or something has gone horribly wrong. It also implies a lack of long-term perspective. Life is long. Sometimes children finding their own way come back to the church eventually, especially if they are treated with kindness and acceptance during their time away. The people who use this saying are well-meaning, but in essence it is a form of coercion to get your children to act how you want them to. Bryan and I had decided long ago that instead of having a family motto centered on no empty chairs in heaven, we would focus on having no empty chairs at our earthly table. We wanted everyone in our family to feel comfortable with us and accepted by us, not judged for their actions or for who they are. We didn't care what the church told us to do, we were going to keep our children close.

Needless to say, I was not distressed by Brooke's answer. I understood that, in general, many people do not have the same interest in the church that I have, and I could especially understand why an LGBTQ person would not want to be involved. I was happy to set Brooke free of the restrictions of the church. I felt calm and comfortable with the idea that she would not participate in or be a part of the church anymore. But of course, there was that nagging thought in the back of my mind that I should care more, I should be more distressed. If I were a true believer, I would strongly desire that my family, as well as everyone else in the world, join and stay in the church.

My conversation with Brooke that day continued for most of the drive time to Brighter Days. We talked about who else knew (Kaitlin and Brooke's friends, including Gwen and Sam) and if she was okay with me telling other family members (yes, she was). By the time I dropped her off, I was dying to talk to Bryan. I called him on my way home, and luckily, he had a patient cancellation, so he could talk for a minute. He was happy to know that Brooke had finally come out to us. Like me, he was not surprised that she didn't want to be part of the church. He was okay with her not going to church on Sunday with us or to any church activities. As he would say often in the coming months, when you pick your child up off the floor from an overdose, your priorities change. We didn't care if she was involved in the church; we wanted her to stay alive and to feel better.

"I guess we will need to use they/them pronouns for Brooke," I said toward the end of the conversation.

"Yes," Bryan replied, "that will be difficult."

"Well," I tried to be upbeat, "we can think of it as a mental challenge, a new thing to learn. It will take time, but we will get used to it."

As I drove the rest of the way home, I contemplated how that sentiment was true not only of the pronoun usage, but of our new reality in general: LGBTQ children, serious mental health challenges, members of the family not in the church. It would take getting used to.

Later that week I made another round of phone calls: to my mom, my dad, and each of my two brothers. I wanted to let them know about Brooke's gender identity and sexual orientation. We also told Mike and Josie, and Haley and Sydney (and we told Kaitlin that Brooke had come out to us). Everyone was kind and understanding, but somewhat confused by the terms. Non-binary gender identification (also known as gender neutral or gender nonconforming) is a novel concept for people of my generation and older. It can be hard to understand and take in, but they were willing to try.

As I spoke with my family, I thought about how I had spent many years wishing they were religious like me and thinking that I would be happier if we were all in the church together. Liz, my life coach, helped me see that this was just a story that my brain had come up with, and that holding on to the story created emotional pain. I was thankful that she helped me see my family in a new way so I could enjoy them more. How ironic that now I was *glad* they weren't religious. Religious conservatives are generally judgmental and intolerant of LGBTQ people (and many other minorities). If my parents were in the church, they would have taken the news of Brooke's identity as a hardship. But as it was, they did not judge; they asked how I felt about it and chose to see it in the same way that I did: something new to learn about and get accustomed to, but nothing shameful or overly problematic.

CHAPTER 11

Ready to Let Go

Getting comfortable using they/them pronouns for Brooke was challenging, but I was committed to making the change. You don't use someone's pronouns when you speak to the person, you use them more when talking to someone else about the person. This came up most often when Bryan and I would talk together about Brooke. At first, we would say "she" and then a few seconds later realize the mistake and repeat the sentence with "they." This is how habits are altered: corrections afterwards at first, and then eventually the new word becomes natural. I started off at about 30 percent accuracy for the correct pronouns and worked up from there. When we were together as a family, all of us made an effort to use Brooke's pronouns. I felt thankful that the kids were supportive and willing to make this adjustment. I would feel a special pride when I used the preferred pronouns in family conversations in front of Brooke, hoping they noticed and felt validated.

The pronouns also came up when talking to non-family members about Brooke. For example, I had to refer to Brooke when I called for their doctor appointments, when I picked up their prescriptions, or when someone asked how they were doing. I often hesitated, pausing to ask myself, should I explain their gender and use they/them to refer to Brooke? Should I not explain but still use the pronouns? Or should I make it easier on myself and others and use she/her? At different times I chose differently. I started referring to Brooke as my child instead of my daughter and used their name more often to avoid the use of pronouns altogether.

In the beginning, I felt nervous bringing it up with others, especially in our conservative, religious community. I didn't know if people would understand or be sympathetic. A lot of my apprehension came from not wanting to make other people uncomfortable. Eventually I decided that their comfort was not that important, certainly not more important than Brooke's comfort. Even if Brooke wasn't present when I choose which pronouns to use, by using they/them, I advocated for non-binary people in general. When people found out that our family had a non-binary child, and that we supported the use of the new pronouns, it would stick with them and let them know that LGBTQ people are common and should be accepted.

When I did use Brooke's preferred pronouns, people would often get confused. They would ask, "Do you have twins?" Or they thought I was talking about Brooke and Sydney. It took patience and repeated clarification, but it was worth it. To keep the new pronouns in the forefront of my mind, I changed Brooke's contact name in my phone to "Brooke (they/them) Hoelzer." When I texted with friends or family about Brooke, I sometimes began the conversation with those pronouns in parentheses, as a reminder. It meant a lot to me when a friend used the pronouns in text replies. I knew it was different and hard, and I appreciated their efforts.

Occasionally, doubts about they/them pronouns crept into my mind. Do we really need to do this? At times I thought it was weird, different, and uncomfortable. My mind kept going back to the idea that it was incorrect grammar. I wondered why the community hadn't come up with a new singular pronoun for non-binary people, like zhe. That would be easier. I came to find out that new pronouns have in fact been suggested and temporarily used, but they did not gain widespread consensus. I didn't want to have reservations about the pronouns; I wanted to embrace the idea without qualms.

One day, I came across an Instagram video that alleviated my questioning. I had started following LGBTQ accounts to learn more about this population. Because of that, Instagram suggested I might like to follow Jeffery Marsh, a popular non-binary influencer who helps people understand LGBTQ issues. In their unique and soothing voice, they explained,

> You know, the thing about the singular they is that it's already been decided. If you're just finding out and you're just objecting, you're objecting to years and years of tradition within our movement. It's

> in the Oxford English Dictionary; it's in Merriam Webster; yes, all of that. But in addition, we've been using it for ourselves for years. It's time to give up your objections and to use it.

This video hit me with such power; it was as if they spoke directly to me. I'm the one just finding out, just objecting. *It's been decided.* Let go of the objections. From that moment on, I relinquished my reluctance. This is a thing; it's here to stay.

Brooke stopped going to church youth activities during the week and did not attend church with Sydney, Bryan, and me on Sundays. I didn't like leaving them home alone while we went off to church together. Now that they didn't go, I thought more and more about staying home myself. Earlier that year, Bryan had suggested that I try "floating"—doing only the church things I wanted to do and not worrying about the rest. He speculated that people could get too focused on the small tasks and lose track of the greater good of religion. By floating, you can take a step back and gain perspective about what's important.

I had adopted this strategy. Since that time, I kept a running list of what isn't required if you float: you don't have to read scriptures on your own or with your family, fast once a month, visit a lonely person you were assigned to go see, refrain from shopping or entertainment on Sundays, have a responsibility or position in the church, try to get people to join or come back to the church, listen or pay attention during classes or lessons. Taking a break from these things was a relief, but it had the opposite effect of what Bryan proposed. Instead of feeling more comfortable and enjoying the parts of the church that were left, it focused my attention on how many things I didn't want to participate in. The list grew longer and longer. It felt nice to not have those obligations.

I had learned from my coach, Liz, that the "shoulds" of our lives create unnecessary guilt and disgrace. The more we think we *should* be doing something, the more shame we generate, the worse we feel about ourselves, and the less motivation we have to do that thing. The brain thinks this judgment and criticism are useful, but it's the opposite. When we have compassion for ourselves, acknowledge the reality, and say, "This is what I *should* be doing right now, because I *am* doing it," then we can use that self-love to activate a desire to do and be better. Although it's non-intuitive, the best way to change yourself is to love yourself however you are.

When I learned about this, I was stunned to recognize how the rules and standards of the church result in an intense environment of shoulds. It is human nature to find fault with yourself, of course; non-religious people still create shame and guilt for themselves. But being part of a religion takes it up a notch. There were so many ways to mess up, so many ways to be and do the wrong thing. There was so little grace for and acceptance of weaknesses and shortcomings. Even though the doctrine taught that Christ offered love and forgiveness and grace, the demanding culture of the church fostered judgment of yourself and others. There were some families who had it "all": job success and affluence, happy marriage, successful children who stayed in the church. The natural conclusion was if your life doesn't look like this, you're doing something wrong.

I was ready to let go of the shoulds and move into self-approval. My depression developed because of my powerful dislike of myself and my alleged weaknesses. I was tired of berating myself and spiraling into crying spasms. I yearned to release those stories. One of my favorite new concepts from Liz was formed as a question: "Why does it not matter that I have weaknesses and shortcomings?" I was trying to trust that this is what it's like to be human; we identify faults in ourselves and magnify them in our minds. This feels important, but that focus is damaging. I wanted to adopt the thought "I am not expected to be perfect" and practice radical self-acceptance.

In addition, I had grown tired of the shoulds the church encouraged for my kids. I was weary of the rules I felt compelled to enforce for them. I wondered if my and Bryan's diligence in teaching our children the tenets of our religion had contributed to Brooke's depression and suicide attempt. Had we unknowingly made Brooke feel distressed and inadequate? The church guidelines seemed to engender disapproval, judgment, and disconnection between me and my kids. I didn't want to participate in that anymore.

For many years, I had been focused on and worried about minor issues like the length of my girls' shorts, the modesty of their swimsuits, or their desire to get too many piercings. I fretted about whether they actively engaged in their church lessons and responsibilities and if they would continue to live the church standards when they were on their own. Even after Kaitlin got married and Haley moved out for college, I mentally monitored their clothes, their Sunday activities, and their level of church participation. I felt like I sent a message of "if only you were slightly different, I could love and accept you fully." I didn't want to live in fear and concern anymore; I wanted to feel unqualified love for them however they chose to live their lives.

So far, Kaitlin and Brooke were choosing to live their lives differently from what Bryan and I had hoped for them. For a long time, we had held onto the dream that we would all be together in the church. That was the ideal and the definition of success that we had been exposed to since our youth. We had been confident that if we worked hard enough, we could achieve that dream. The idealized version of our family was now crumbling, and we had a choice: be mournful about that and disengage from those two children or let go of our previous story and accept our new reality. I had learned from Liz that when we hold on to a narrative of how we believe our families or our lives should be, we miss out on the experience in front of us. It's possible that the new version is even better than the old one. It's possible this is the best way for our family to be. I felt such gratitude that Liz had helped me prepare my mind for this change in our family. She helped me see that my tight grip on the story of how we should look didn't serve me or my family. It was a relief to loosen that grip.

Bryan did not have as easy of a time letting go of the dream. He still wished we could all be at church together; part of him still thought that was the best way for our family. He was raised by a single mom and had a lot of instability in his early years. Later, when his family became more involved in the church, his life began to have more steadiness. In his mind, the structure and order of the church resulted in a more predictable life. He liked the idea that if you did A and B, you would get C.

He believed in the church doctrines, but he also liked the image of success that a family in the church portrayed. He had been successful in many parts of his life, he wanted to triumph in this area too. Sometimes I related to that. Occasionally, my brain still offered me the thought that I would be happier or that it would be better if we were all in the church. But I recognized that as a story I made up and could choose to hold on to and create pain for myself if I desired. I had learned to talk back to my brain when it offered me such stories. In those moments, I would reply, "You can think that if you want to, but it is not *truth*, and it will not create the result you seek, which is love and connection with your family."

Another thing Bryan wasn't ready to relinquish was his leadership role as president of the men's group. He enjoyed being in charge and getting things done. He excelled at organization and efficiency, as well as at making others feel loved and wanted. He had a knack for creating a feeling of comradery within the group. He felt helpful and useful, and he liked receiving praise for his efforts. As president, he attended a meeting twice a month with the leaders of the other groups where they coordinated their service efforts, planned activities, and shared information about any members who were struggling. He felt uplifted after these meetings. He got to be involved and know what was happening in our congregation, and he saw the great things members were doing for each other.

I also enjoyed many aspects of leadership roles, including the information sharing and the planning and executing of ideas. But I supposed that if I didn't live the standards (because I was "floating"), and if I didn't believe fully in the views of the church, then I shouldn't get the benefit of holding a leadership position. I felt increasingly out of place at church. My personality tends toward an all-or-nothing perspective, and that's how I see the principles of the church: you attempt to do all of it, or you aren't a true member. It's not as if I fervently believed but couldn't complete the tasks and expectations. I consciously decided not to do those things. In truth, I questioned whether those things were even worth doing.

Additionally, doubts crept in for me around the concept of judgment. The logic of assigning people to heaven or hell after they die based on their character and their actions on Earth started to unravel for me. Judgment, of course, is a hallmark of religion in general and Christianity in particular. Preachers and pastors have leaned heavily on this concept to inspire righteous behavior in their congregants, including the paying of tithes and offerings. Christians have talked about judgment and damnation since the time of Christ. When you imagine you are on the correct side of this equation (you're going to heaven because you believed and did the right things), this concept is comforting. It feels good to know you are headed toward celestial exaltation, and it also feels kind of good to believe that others aren't. Humans compare themselves to others and have a strong desire to be better than someone else. We are acutely aware of our own shortcomings, so we take comfort in thinking others have even more faults. With their rules and ideas about what's good and bad, Christians are especially primed to look around, find fault with others, and feel superior.

In Jim Gaffigan's special *Mr. Universe*, he talks about his love of McDonald's. He says he likes to tell people that he eats at McDonald's because they get a look on their faces like,

"Oh, I didn't know I was better than you." Christians experience that type of superiority when they see someone who isn't a believer or who has left the church or who struggles at being "righteous." When you're taught consistently that you must do these things to be in God's favor and to achieve salvation, it's impossible not to use that yardstick against others. The more strongly you feel that this is true, the less compassion you have for other people's shortcomings. Yes, we're taught to have mercy and grace for others, but we're not good at it, and when we are, it can come off as condescending.

The more I learned about the world and about human psychology, the less I believed in a post mortal judgment. If there was such an assessment, it would have to include a lot of mercy because people are highly influenced by their genetic makeup and their family, social, and political environments. We like to think of people as being good or bad, or even their actions as good or bad, but life is not that simple. In the big picture of human behavior, there are broad patterns of how humans respond in certain settings. For example, oppressed groups tend to react in predictable ways to their difficult conditions, ways others often see as self-defeating or slothful. However, studies of human behavior indicate that almost all people would act in a similar manner if placed in the same situation and surroundings. Another example is when people gain positions of power. We think they are greedy or conniving, but maybe this is a natural consequence of being human. We can judge others' conduct, but that is naïve. It's impossible to know how we would behave in a circumstance until we are faced with it.

People have reasons for how they operate. When you learn more about their personal history and current circumstances, you realize that what you see as weakness, error, or sin is people truly functioning to the best of their ability. If we are honest with ourselves, we can see that we might have responded in the same way. Personality is less concrete than we like to think. Studies have shown that when people are put in particular settings, they act the same, regardless of their previous traits. Many times, we think we make a choice, but actually we enact patterns of human behavior that have been seen throughout time.

In her coaching program, Liz suggested we choose to imagine that everyone is doing the best they can. Of course, this can never be proven one way or another, but I decided to adamantly believe it. Every person is doing their best, given their genetics, their current physiology, the environment they grew up in, and the situation at hand. We don't always understand why they behave in certain ways, but believing they are doing their best brings up compassion and curiosity rather than criticism and judgment.

Choosing to assume this changed my view of the world. I had half-believed this before, but I still saw some people as inherently "bad," especially extreme cases such as criminals or dictators. When you narrow in on someone's life, however, and find out what they've been through, their conduct makes more sense. This doesn't mean that we condone the behavior or let it go without consequences. It means that we take away the judgment part. We believe they did their best, and we attempt to find a solution to the problem or a way to help them behave better in the future.

The result of believing that everyone is doing their best is that you cannot also believe in a post-mortal judgment. Who goes to heaven and who goes to hell? Consider two children in elementary school. One sits still at her desk and listens, obeys instructions, and does her work quietly. The other bounces around, talking to classmates and being disruptive. Is the second child "bad?" Why is he acting that way? Does he want to be bad? Is it possible that he has not learned the correct way to act? Is it possible that with his biochemistry it is difficult to sit still? Should the first child be rewarded for behaviors that come naturally to her? It's not like she has the same tendencies as the second child but uses willpower to overcome them. Being quiet, listening, and obeying are effortless for her. She shouldn't be rewarded any more than the other child should be punished. From this perspective, the idea of a simple and final judgment becomes harder to accept.

It is easy for Christians to look at others and condemn their bad behavior. This tendency comes from a lack of understanding about other people's situations and what motivates behavior, as well as a self-righteous belief that they know what the correct behavior is. That piety was slipping through my hands. I no longer believed that we Christians cornered the market on morality, that we make the rules about what's acceptable to God and what's not. My view of the world had expanded to include different types of people and to let go of judgment about the way those people lived their lives. If you don't believe in judgment or a heaven/hell afterlife, it is hard to remain Christian. You no longer trust that you need to do any of the other things the church commands you to do.

These ideas had been swimming through my mind over the last year. I already had one foot out the door of the church, and when Brooke told us about their identity, that gave me another nudge. However, I didn't want to make an important decision while at the bottom of the U-curve of happiness. I thought maybe my current stage of adult development might be related to my disaffection for the church. Maybe I should wait until my mid-fifties and then see if I still wanted to leave. But I had fewer and fewer reasons to stay. Leaving Brooke behind when we attended church services felt like a betrayal, like I sided with the anti-LGBTQ church and not with Brooke.

I knew that the doctrine of our church had always excluded LGBTQ people. Its tenets say that God only approves of marriage between a man and a woman and that you must be married to qualify for the highest level of heaven. In addition, the church teaches that gender is an essential characteristic of your eternal being, and there are only two genders. Like many Christian churches, my denomination had changed its rhetoric about homosexuality over the decades. In the 1960s, being gay was deemed deviant and subversive, something sinful people chose to participate in. Until 1973, homosexuality was a diagnosis in the psychiatric diagnostic manual (DSM), and therefore considered to be a mental health condition. Conversion therapy and electroshock therapy were common treatments for gay people.

In the 1990s, my church started calling homosexuality "same-sex attraction." They used this term in ways that still implied it was an affliction to be overcome. They likened it to other temptations: if you prayed hard enough and stayed obedient to the rules, you will receive divine help to get past the enticements. At this time, Christian churches acknowledged that being gay was genetic or inherent and was not going to change or be "fixed" (although conversion therapy continued for decades beyond this). Church leaders encouraged members to love and accept gay people (hate the sin, love the sinner), but they admonished gay followers to obey the standards of chastity, which state that sex is only approved between a man and woman after they are married. This meant that gay members had to be alone and celibate for the duration of their lives. Another option my church championed was "mixed-orientation marriages." Gay men were told to marry a woman and make it work. Both these alternatives are extremely harmful to the mental health of gay people, not to mention the heterosexual spouse in the mixed-orientation marriage. Another insidious idea suggested to gay people was that they will be "cured" in the next life.

In the past, I understood that these principles were hurtful to people who did not fit the straight, cis-gender mold. But I had been able to put that aside and focus on the many ways the church benefited our family. The church brought us together every Sunday for services and every evening for scripture study. I cherished this time with my family and felt that it would be difficult to gather the kids so often without such a compelling reason. Church teachings helped us focus on gratitude and serving others. The rules and standards brought structure and discipline to our lives, which appealed to my personality. The church encouraged us to give our time and money to benefit others. It helped us remember and take courage from those who had gone before us and suffered hardships. Many of these concepts have been studied and identified in the field of positive psychology as promoting happiness. Those of us in the church had a head start on these behaviors.

However, now the church's LGBTQ policies hit closer to home. I could not look the other way so easily. Leaving Brooke at home to attend church seemed like an indication that I espoused those doctrines.

I followed an Instagram account that served as a support group for religious families with LGBTQ children. Once a week, they highlighted a family with an LGBTQ child. As I read these stories, I noticed a pattern. The child recognizes his identity around age eleven or twelve. Throughout his youth, he sits in church meetings and hears teachings about how gay behavior is a sin and there are only two genders. He learns that if he is gay or trans, he will not make it to heaven and his family will be upset because he is missing. He internalizes these ideas and concludes that he is terrible, wicked, and not worthy of heaven. The child assumes his family believes what the church teaches. He imagines that his family wouldn't want him around if they knew and that he must choose between his family and his identity. Many of these children are deeply religious and want to know of God's love for them and feel acceptable before Him, in addition to wishing their family would be supportive of their identities. Not surprisingly, these children often suffer from depression, anxiety, and panic attacks. Many of them contemplate or attempt suicide. They think, "If I will be fixed in the next life, maybe I should go there now."

As I read story after story like this, I felt sick. These were tragic tales of pain and suffering that didn't have to be. Ironically, in most of the stories, when the youth finally told his parents, they were accepting and loving. They either separated from the church eventually or felt considerably conflicted about staying. The parents often scoffed at the idea that the only two choices the church presented their gay child were a lonely life of celibacy or expulsion from the church. Why shouldn't their child get to participate in the full spectrum of human experiences, including intimacy? These parents allowed their child to stop attending church because they recognized that they would do the same if their heterosexual desires were deemed "against God's will." But as the kids struggled with their identities in their teen years, they didn't know this. They assumed their parents would hate them or want nothing to do with them. To prevent this, the parents could have said, early on, "Even though the church teaches such-and-such, if you have one of these identities, we will accept you."

Why do parents in the church not say this to their kids? They worry that announcing acceptance of LGBTQ identities increases the chances their kids will eventually become part of the LGBTQ community. Also, if their children don't identify that way, the parents don't want to unnecessarily communicate to their kids that they don't believe the church doctrines. They want to look like faithful, committed members. They hold a secret hope that they won't have to deal with this sticky issue. I know I did.

CHAPTER 12

Redoing the Family Timeline

Christmas that year was different from any other year, not only because of the somber mood that still pervaded our house, but also because we were missing some family members. Haley wasn't there (missionaries don't come home for holidays), and Kaitlin and Ben had flown to Minnesota to be with Ben's family for the holiday. That left Bryan, Brooke, Sydney, and me. We still did our usual Christmas Eve traditions, including making sugar cookies, holding a religious family devotional, serving tortellini with red and green sauce for dinner, and going on a treasure hunt to find the only gift the kids get to open that night: matching pajamas. We always have a photo shoot in the new pajamas, and the kids (not "girls" anymore) love to model for it. We have a display of these photos from over the years as part of our Christmas decorations. This year, Brooke and Sydney were the only ones in the pictures. We sent the pictures to Kaitlin and Haley, letting them know we missed them. The celebrations were smaller and quieter than usual but fun, nonetheless.

Brooke continued to go to day treatment over winter break, every day except Christmas Eve, Christmas Day, and New Year's Day. I felt relieved that they continued the program. Brooke was doing well there, and I wasn't ready to have them home all day. The psychiatrist who supervised the program had met with Brooke and increased their dosage of Zoloft. However, we were still waiting to see the mood-improving effects. We continued to ask Brooke their "numbers" nightly, and the depression number never got below six. I spoke with the psychiatrist, and he agreed with our concerns about Brooke's depression not lifting appreciably. He said he would wait a few more weeks and then consider switching to another medication in the antidepressant family.

After the first week of the program, Brooke didn't have any more instances of self-harm. When we asked for their update each night, however, the desire to self-harm number was often high. We discussed how that felt and what other coping skills they could employ to distract themself.

Brooke went to day treatment without objection, but they did have complaints about how it was run. They said that it was disorganized, and time was often wasted. They didn't like their therapist, Jill, or the other staff members. Brooke had connected with the therapist at the inpatient unit, and we lamented that it couldn't be the other way around—the more impactful therapist at the place Brooke spent the most time. But I reassured myself that the universe is constantly conspiring in our favor. Many times, we can't see it, or it doesn't make sense to us. Things were supposed to go this way.

I had disappointments of my own with the program. In the registration process, the intake counselor said the program leaders would enroll Brooke in school and keep them going on their studies. Three hours a day were set aside for the kids to do schoolwork. Day after day, I would ask Brooke about this, and they would say that the teacher was still getting them registered or there wasn't any work to do that day. I wasn't too worried about it because I knew Brooke had plenty of time in their senior year of high school to get enough credits for graduation. But I was frustrated that Brooke played solitaire on the computer or napped for three hours a day. Eventually, I gave up hope that any schoolwork would be done. I worked with Brooke's counselor at their regular school to have them unenrolled for that term and not receive any credit. This was better than having Fs show up on the transcript, which would have happened since the day treatment program never transferred Brooke's enrollment to their school.

My other dissatisfaction was with the group therapy. The initial program information indicated that the mental health professionals do Dialectical Behavior Therapy (DBT) with the youth. I had not heard of DBT; it became mainstream after I completed my social work training. I researched it and thought it seemed like an effective mode of treatment. DBT is an outgrowth of cognitive-behavioral therapy and has a lot in common with that modality. Dialectical is an unfamiliar word, but it means holding two opposing ideas at the same time. Human minds favor extremes and tend to think in black and white terms. It takes maturity and training to consider the nuance of situations. DBT teaches clients the strategies to do that. Through the skills modules of DBT, clients learn emotion regulation, distress tolerance, mindfulness, and interpersonal effectiveness. The goal is to help individuals accept and tolerate powerful emotions that come up when they challenge their habits or expose themselves to distressing situations. There is a large educational component to DBT, with many new concepts and acronyms to learn.

I thought this sounded wonderful and efficacious. In the first week of day treatment, Brooke came home with a large binder full of DBT lessons and modules. I was full of hope and excitement. But after a few days, they left the binder at home. I asked about it, and Brooke said they never used it and rarely talked about DBT. I felt disheartened but chose to trust the professionals of the program. I reminded myself that this was a short period in Brooke's life; I tried to not magnify the importance of these few weeks. Our main goal was to have time pass so the medication would start working. If Brooke learned anything useful along the way, all the better. Maybe what Brooke was learning included how to be patient with an unproductive program and how to interact with others whom they didn't care for. These were useful lessons even if my mind would have preferred a "perfect" experience for Brooke.

Gwen moved back home over Christmas break. For reasons unknown to me, her parents decided that she could come back, even though they had planned on her being away the rest of the school year. Brooke was elated, and I was relieved. I knew this didn't mean things would be perfect, but Brooke was happier when Gwen was around. They hung out together when they could over the break. Brooke missed out on some social activities because of day treatment, but I felt fine with the tradeoff.

Brooke's program required weekly family therapy sessions, and Bryan and I complied happily. The therapist, Jill, didn't think the siblings needed to be involved, only the parents. The weekly Zoom call included Bryan, Jill, Brooke, and me. We held it on Thursdays over Bryan's lunch hour and discussed whatever topic Jill proposed. After the initial introductory meeting, Jill assigned Bryan and me to write "impact statements" to be read in future sessions. We were to describe the impact that Brooke's actions had on us. I felt uncertain about this task because I don't believe that outside events cause feelings. Brooke didn't "make" me feel upset or scared or disappointed. I create my own emotions and knowing this helps me get leverage over them and not give my power away to someone or something else. I explained that in my statement but still detailed what I felt over the course of Brooke's hospitalization. I realized that the purpose of the exercise was to help the youth see the experience through another person's perspective, and I figured that was a useful endeavor.

In the family therapy sessions, I had my first opportunities to use Brooke's they/them pronouns. I felt clumsy and self-conscious at first. But talking to Jill about Brooke provided a forum to get accustomed to speaking in this new way and to show Brooke my commitment to them. Bryan was confused at first about whom I referred to when I said "they," and he told me later he was impressed with my efforts and ability to change my habits and accommodate Brooke's desire so quickly.

Our next family therapy assignment was to write a one- to two-page autobiography. Jill encouraged us to talk about our childhood struggles and triumphs and to open up about other problems or difficulties we had dealt with in our lives. Brooke wrote one also, and we read them in turns during our subsequent meetings. I wrote mine easily; I knew I wanted to share more about myself than I had previously with Brooke. I labored to maintain my composure when I read it. I talked about viewing myself as a negative, unloving person. The vignettes I gave seemed trivial when read aloud, but they are painful to me. I wanted to show Brooke that I was willing to go through that awkwardness and exertion to bring us closer and to be more open. Bryan did the same. He talked about the painful childhood experiences of his parents' divorce, his mom's remarriage, and the subsequent blending of two families. He emphasized the strengths that he had built as he overcame those adversities, such as his charming sense of humor.

Brooke felt sheepish sharing their autobiography because they felt like we already knew about their life. They had written about their childhood and school experiences, and indeed, it was mostly information we were familiar with. In the following week, I thought about the assignment and felt we had missed an opportunity. I emailed Jill and asked if she'd consider having Brooke write another autobiography, this time focusing on their nonbinary and bisexual identities. This was a part of Brooke that I didn't already know and urgently wanted to understand. Jill agreed that it was a good idea. I felt the universe had inspired me with this thought because their second autobiography revealed much more.

On the appointed day, we gathered on the Zoom call. Bryan sat in his office at work, and I was in my home office. The sun shone brightly through the window and onto the snow-covered front yard. Brooke and Jill connected from the computer in Jill's office. I liked getting this peek into her office. She had motivational posters on the wall and some boxes stacked behind the desk. Brooke sat to the side and slightly behind Jill and fiddled with the papers in their lap as we exchanged pleasantries. Eventually, Jill turned to Brooke and asked them to share their second autobiography.

The beginning line they read stated, "When I was a child, I always felt like I was different." This surprised me. As I've mentioned, Brooke was such a happy, easy-going, pleasant child. I assumed that's how they felt on the inside too. But they told a different story. They talked about not having or even wanting friends in elementary school, asking to stay inside for recess to help the teacher and somehow knowing that was strange. They did say that their overall emotion during childhood was contentment, but that they didn't feel connected to any friends and preferred to play by themself. They also related that they never felt comfortable being a girl. Again, news to me. My mind reviewed the dresses and girly outfits I'd chosen for Brooke as a young child, and I squirmed in my seat.

Brooke then talked about the internalized pressure they felt as a child to always be the good kid, the one who didn't need help in school, didn't get upset, and always remained even-tempered. They surmised that this pressure led to suppressing emotions and not learning how to deal with them. They felt in the shadows at times, like they were not important and their problems were not real.

In middle school, they began to question their sexuality. They wrote: "I remember learning what a lesbian is in like 6/7 grade and thinking, 'wait, that's allowed?!' very happily." Brooke continued to feel a disconnection from their assigned gender and a general feeling of wrongness that they couldn't understand. They had heard about nonbinary as a gender identity but didn't understand it. Then something changed all that. In their sophomore year, Gwen came out to Brooke as nonbinary and wanted to use they/them pronouns and a new name, Star. This "opened up a whole new, very freeing world" for Brooke.

In the autobiography they said, "I thought about it for a long time because it was scary to me, and I wanted to deny it, but somewhere I knew. I think without Star, it would've taken me longer to realize and to accept myself but knowing and being out is a huge blessing and is so liberating."

Recently, Brooke had come out to Star about being nonbinary, and they cherished Star's support and approval. Brooke read from their papers, "Accepting myself as trans is one of the hardest things I've done, but it's [so] worth it." The autobiography stated that Brooke wanted to come out to us and didn't think we'd be mad, but they weren't sure what we'd think and didn't want to have the hard conversations.

At the end of the letter, Brooke addressed religion and the church. They said, "Being queer definitely put me at odds with religion, but I think even without that I would've left the church. I'm not a fan of organized religion, but recently I've been getting into spirituality which seems like a good thing in my life, and I'm glad I have parents who support that." It felt good to know that Brooke was happy with our reaction. I wasn't surprised about their lack of religiosity. I had sensed that Brooke didn't have the verve and zest of a devoted church member.

I appreciated this added insight into Brooke's experience, and when I talked to Bryan later, he heartily agreed. Brooke had many thoughts and feelings that we didn't know about. I didn't blame myself for my ignorance because I felt like we had done the best we could, but gaining this new perspective was helpful. It makes a difference when you hear someone describe their experience in their own words. I had a greater understanding of Brooke now. I felt a rush of gratitude toward Gwen (now Star). Their friendship and support of Brooke meant a lot to me. Brooke was lucky to have such a person in their life. I was ready to embrace Star's name, identity, and pronouns as fully as I had embraced Brooke's.

After Brooke read their autobiography in the family therapy session, Jill helped us discuss it. We asked some questions, and we expressed our empathy at what Brooke had gone through. We tried to be supportive and let them know that we love them and that learning more about them doesn't change that. In fact, it helps our love grow stronger. We felt delighted to get to know the real Brooke, and we knew that our relationship would be closer because of this openness and sharing.

We asked Brooke what they would have done if none of this had ever come out. They said they figured they would leave the house after high school and not be a part of the family anymore. They thought their lifestyle might be unacceptable to us (not just the LGBTQ identities, but also the piercings and tattoos and outfits they planned to have), and we wouldn't want them around. This broke our hearts, obviously. How could Brooke think that we would want them to stay away? But when you think of what we had taught our kids through the years and our close affiliation with the church, I guess it makes sense. Bryan and I hoped that through this process of getting to know the real Brooke and being more open about our own struggles, we would show them that they were more important to us than the doctrines of the church.

Being more open with the kids about our struggles is something Bryan and I talked about a lot during this time. We didn't have marital conflict, but we both battled personal crises. Mine had to do with depression caused by my changing life roles and my perceived weaknesses and shortcomings. Bryan struggled to get used to the changes that came with moving and starting a new job. We were open with each other and found great strength from talking things through together. We did not talk about these issues with our kids, though. For them, we wanted to be positive. We didn't think it was appropriate or necessary to tell them our challenges. If I'm upset and about to cry (a not-uncommon occurrence), I will leave the situation, go to my room, and let it out. I feel like I should hide these negative emotions from my children. Once I picked Haley up from a dance class, and I felt upset and on the verge of tears. I knew I couldn't talk without crying, so I didn't talk the whole way home. I practically held my breath and didn't make any eye contact during the drive. Looking back, that seems silly. Of course, she knew something was wrong. Why not express my feelings, talk about what's bothering me, and let her see me cry?

I kept coming back to what Haley had brought up last summer. Living with Amanda's family briefly, she saw how open they were with each other, and she wanted us to be more like that. I thought about how we didn't want Kaitlin to discuss her medications with her siblings or with others, and how I asked her not to tell her siblings when she came out to us as bisexual. I saw how I tried to hold those things away from our family. They didn't fit the image I wanted to create and project. I had an idea of how we should look, and I had to push out what was really happening to maintain that illusion.

In December, Bryan and I met with a therapist together to make sure we were dealing with the strain of recent events. Even though we only had two sessions, our therapist mentioned something that stuck with us. As we talked about our interactions with our children and Brooke's acknowledgement that they suppressed emotion to appear like the "good kid," he commented that maybe our kids felt held to an elevated standard of behavior, particularly when it came to handling challenging emotions. If we never talked with them about our difficulties, they possibly assumed that we didn't have any, and by extension, that they shouldn't have any, either. We had given the impression that success means not having any problems, instead of showing them that our success came from working through our problems.

The therapist also pointed out that our children see our accomplishments in marriage and vocations, but, he asked, have we ever talked about the labors it took to achieve those goals? It might look to them like we always had those things and that they came easily. They didn't necessarily recognize the hard work it took to attain our marital, financial, and emotional stability. Without knowing this, they might infer that the effort they exert to achieve the same things implies that something has gone wrong.

This is not the message we intended to give, of course. When I questioned why I didn't talk about my troubles with my kids, I realized that it was partly because of my story that I was a negative person, and therefore I needed to go the extra mile to be positive. Also, I wanted to give the impression that we could deal successfully with any setbacks. I didn't want them to see the mess, the personal frustrations, and the disappointments. I thought that by concealing that part, they could avoid it. I see now how this could backfire and lead children to erroneous conclusions.

As 2020 ended, Bryan and I brainstormed ways we could change that. We decided to hold weekly family meetings on Sunday nights, starting in January. In these meetings, Bryan and I would talk about our problems—all our problems. We announced this plan to our kids and arranged for Haley to join through video chat. The kids were intrigued and excited; Bryan and I felt jittery and awkward.

We began by expressing more of our frustrations with our own families while growing up. Our kids knew a bit about this, but we had always downplayed our disappointments so that our children wouldn't have negative opinions about their extended relatives. We threw that idea out the window. We let loose with how we felt, but still acknowledged that this was our interpretation and that everyone has reasons for what they do. It wasn't, "I'll tell you how terrible this person was," but more, "look at how I allowed that to bother me." We acknowledged that, yes, we get frustrated by other people and we feel disappointed in ourselves, sometimes to the point where it interferes with our functioning.

We talked about the struggles in our marriage and the hard work it took for Bryan to get through medical school and residency (and for me to take care of the kids during those years). I told them more details about my parents' divorce and the distress that caused me. I revealed what Brooke already knew from my autobiography, the stories I carry around about being too negative and the depression those stories created. Bryan related how he often ruminates about what might have been and how that prevents him from enjoying the present. For example, his constant thought, "If I had stayed at my old job, I wouldn't be dealing with this problem," took away from any joy he might feel regarding the positive aspects of his new job.

These meetings continued weekly into March. We had a lot of material to unload on them. Not surprisingly, the kids were fascinated by these stories. They were not disappointed in us or concerned for us. We became real people. Everyone discovers this at some point about their parents; we helped our kids see it sooner rather than later, and we gave them a forum to discuss it with us. The meetings were a huge success.

When we finished sharing our experiences, we asked the kids if they wanted to share. Kaitlin and Haley each took an evening. They went through their mental health journeys, including when their challenges began and what they've done through the years to alleviate the difficulties. I was proud of them for being willing to be open. They clearly had a different idea from me about the necessity of presenting a perfect image. They were great examples for the younger two.

As we neared the end of these meetings, Bryan had a brilliant idea to sum them up. Every year around the time of our anniversary in October, we helped the kids create a timeline of our family. Only happy occasions were included, of course: our marriage and college graduations, the births and baptisms of the kids, and more recently, the kids' graduations and marriages. This activity reviewed important events and built family unity.

Bryan proposed that we redo the family timeline, and this time include *all* the events that had happened to our family, positive and negative. Right next to Dad starting medical school would be mom going to therapy to deal with her parents' divorce. Before Kaitlin's high school graduation comes Kaitlin going on SSRI medication to manage her anxiety. We taped a piece of yarn down the length of a wall and hung cutout signs of the year and the events that took place that year. It was a true and complete family timeline now, no information withheld or concealed. We felt this new version gave our kids more realistic expectations about the ups and downs of life.

In mid-January, the psychiatrist at Brooke's program recommended that if we didn't see improvement in their mood soon, their medication should be changed. Bryan and I hoped that Brooke could stay on Zoloft because each new medication takes at least two weeks to work. Right around this time, however, a ray of sunshine came shining into the situation. Brooke started to feel better. The shift was subtle, but the depression numbers they reported each evening went down. More importantly, I could see a difference in Brooke's behavior and overall countenance. There was a lightness to their step, an ease in their interactions that I hadn't seen in months. I felt wonderfully relieved—a light at the end of a long tunnel. The doctor was satisfied with the improvement and decided to stay with Zoloft.

Haley's mental health, on the other hand, declined steadily. On her own in New Mexico, she had been having a hard time for months. Shortly after she arrived on her mission, she was assigned to train another new missionary. She did not feel adequate for this responsibility. Her mind constantly told her she wasn't doing enough and wasn't good enough, even though she followed the rules and studied the scriptures and the lesson manuals diligently. We spoke over video chats twice a week, and over time I could see her mood worsening. Sometimes she sat in a corner of her room with no lights on or out on the balcony at night, the hood of her sweatshirt pulled up over her head, obscuring her face. She often cried and said she couldn't manage talking about herself or her life. She wanted me to fill the time chatting about things that had happened at home.

I pined over what to say and how to help her. Bryan knew about Haley's struggles, but because I was home during the day to video chat with her, the bulk of helping her fell on my shoulders. It was agonizing to witness her decreasing ability to function at her usual high capacity. She was paralyzed with the fear of doing the wrong thing. She reported that she cried almost every day. Her roommates were worried about her. At one point, the president asked her to give a three- to five-minute talk at a mission conference. Missionaries do this all the time. It should be easy to prepare and no big deal to give. But Haley felt exceedingly distressed over this assignment. She couldn't think of anything to say and continuously criticized herself and believed that no one wanted to hear from her.

The idea of Haley starting antidepressant medication while on her mission was out of the question. After what had happened to Brooke, I wouldn't take the chance that Haley might feel suicidal and lacked adequate supervision. If she needed medication, she'd have to come home. The mission had a counselor assigned to help missionaries who struggled with mental health problems. Haley had a few sessions with him, but she didn't like him, and he wasn't helpful.

Bryan and I fretted about what to do. Should we encourage Haley to come home? We didn't want to give the impression that she couldn't handle it or that we wanted her to leave. We felt it would be best if she made that decision on her own. On the other hand, we knew she was in a deep depression and probably wouldn't get better if she continued her mission.

Coming home from a mission is a big deal in our community and not a decision to take lightly. Young adults came home primarily for two reasons: serious medical problems or flagrant violations of mission rules. When someone came home, friends and family speculated about which of these two things caused the premature return. Many missionaries felt a sense of shame and guilt if they came home for mental health reasons. We worried that because of this, coming home would only add to Haley's burden.

Haley consulted the president of the mission for advice, but his simple advice was to continue working hard and things would get better. We got the impression that he didn't have much experience with mental health issues. He complimented her hard work and told her to focus on the positive. The summary of his advice was, "Buck up!"

In late February, Haley started to consider leaving her mission. Before she could make the decision, she wanted to feel an answer from God. She contemplated and prayed and read scriptures, but the answer she searched for never came. This reinforced her belief that God didn't approve of her and thought she wasn't good enough. She wrestled with her spirituality and her decision-making abilities in this way for the next few months. We spoke about it during our calls, but because we lived in different states, I felt like I was on the sidelines watching her fight this battle, holding my breath and yearning for any sign of improvement.

CHAPTER 13

A Common Crisis

Our children were not the only late-teens/young adults suffering from depression and anxiety. The number of people in this age group dealing with these problems is staggering. Rates of depression and anxiety have increased steadily over the last few decades. What accounts for this rise?

There is no one answer, of course. We talk about mental health more openly now, and people are more comfortable admitting to emotional struggles. This means that more people get help, and therefore, more people are diagnosed. It could be that this number or percentage of people were always suffering, but we didn't know it before.

Many professionals point to the increased use of electronics and social media as a factor contributing to the escalation of depression and anxiety. Electronic devices themselves may not be detrimental, but the more time youth spend on them, the less time they spend doing other things such as physical or social activity, being outside, or sleeping. Decreasing the time spent on these beneficial activities has a cumulative negative effect on happiness and wellbeing. Because of the prevalence of electronics, youth date less, delay getting their driver's licenses, and in general spend more time in their rooms and less time out in the world.

Using social media has its own harmful consequences. Seeing your friends have fun without you creates loneliness and insecurity. Comparing yourself to others' Instagram moments generates jealousy and dissatisfaction with your own life. The constant need to keep up with Snapchat streaks and group text messages can add internal pressure and anxiety. These are stressors that youth are not ready for or well-equipped to deal with.

The more kids I had in this age category and the more people I spoke with, the more I realized what an epidemic the mental health struggles were becoming for youth. Every family seemed to have at least one child—if not multiple children—dealing with depression and/or anxiety. Many required hospitalizations, as Brooke had. Suicide and suicide attempts were also on the rise. In addition to gathering firsthand accounts, I heard about this nationwide phenomenon from podcasts, news reports, and documentaries. Because of this, I felt less embarrassed about my kids' struggles than I might have. I knew this was a common problem with unknown origins. I wanted to be more open and public about our experiences to normalize mental health struggles and to help others feel less alone.

The statistics show a sharp rise in depression, anxiety, and suicide rates once phone use became the norm for middle schoolers. But the rates started rising even before widespread handheld electronics use. Another causal theory has to do with the body's need to fight against something. A century ago, the main threat to physical health was infectious disease. Microbes entered the body, and the immune system would kick into action to fight them off. Many people died from these infections, obviously, and the advent of antibiotics was revolutionary to public health. But in the decades after antibiotics became common, rates of autoimmune diseases have risen dramatically. It's as if the body needs something to combat, and once the microbes were gone (relatively), it turned against itself.

Mental health is analogous to that. In the past decades our lives have become easier and easier. We have so many conveniences now: climate-controlled living spaces, plenty of food, endless entertainment at our fingertips. Additionally, in recent decades, parenting has shifted to a child-centered approach. Parents spend more time and money on their children because they have fewer of them. We shuttle them around to more activities and buy them more clothes and toys than parents of a previous generation did. Children don't have to share a room with a sibling, or even a bathroom in many cases. In an effort to be "good parents," we often smooth the way, so our children don't have to face problems or uncomfortable situations (a strategy termed *lawn-mower parenting*). Many of the parents of my generation grew up with divorced parents and/or working moms. It seems we want to shield our children from these hardships, even though these difficulties made us strong, capable, and independent. We want our children to have those same traits, but without the struggle.

Because of this ease, our children's brains don't have emotional problems to solve anymore; they don't have any hard situations to push up against. They have the insecurity and malaise that comes from using electronics and participating on social media, but for some reason that doesn't seem to produce the same resilience that sharing your house and your parents' attention with four or five siblings (and other old-fashioned obstacles) create.

Therapists report that their young adult clients get along with their parents and feel accepted and loved by them, for the most part. They have fewer conflicts with parents than clients from two decades ago. But they're still anxious and depressed. It's confusing and frustrating, but it seems that our brains, like our bodies, need to battle against difficulties; we need "problems" to keep us mentally and physically strong.

There's not much we can do about this. No one wants to sign up for a harder life for the off chance that their children might be less depressed or anxious. There's unpleasantness either way. And we may never know if these family conditions do in fact cause our children's mental health crises. It's impossible to prove. It's a theory that makes sense to me, but it breaks down when I apply it to my children. My kids had it easy in some ways, with happily married parents who were attentive and present, a loving stay-at-home mom and an engaged dad, and plenty of food, clothes, and activities. But in other ways they worked hard. All of them studied diligently and earned exceptional grades. They were required to participate in church on Sundays, family scripture reading throughout the week, and other various church activities, which often included service. They had chores around the house, they shared rooms and bathrooms, and they all started working before they turned sixteen. Their lives were not that different from their 1980s equivalents.

However, even though we gave them responsibilities at home and had high expectations in many ways, I must admit, there was a different tone to our parenting than parents of previous generations. As I look back, I can see that we often emphasized fun as the most important element of any activity. We wanted them to be *happy*, and we put no small amount of pressure on them to achieve and maintain that feeling. We told them how much fun we had in high school and implored them to have the same experiences. I noticed that whenever they came home from an activity, my first question was, "Did you have fun?"

In truth, I did want their lives to be easy. I thought that was a sign of good parenting and of successful kids. The recent studies about and popularity of grit and resilience came about too late for my childrearing. If our kids weren't happy or having fun, Bryan and I felt concerned, and we strategized about what we could change in their lives. I didn't have Liz as a coach back then, and I didn't yet understand negative emotion—that it's not a problem to be solved; that it's okay to feel all the emotions, the whole range; that this is what it's like to be human. We create negative emotion for ourselves no matter how advantageous our circumstances appear. The only thing

I knew about negative emotion is that I didn't want it for me or my kids. I made every attempt to ensure that my kids were happy and that they stayed that way. I also sheltered them from painful situations because I wanted them to like me. It felt good to be their protector and savior.

I can see that this approach is different from that of my parents' generation. But it doesn't seem significant enough to create the mental anguish my kids felt from their depression and anxiety. We will never know with certainty what dynamics are responsible for the rise in mental health troubles, and really, once it's there, we don't need to. The treatment for the problem is the same regardless of the cause. We can look forward and not backward and do the best we can in the future.

LGBTQ youth have an even higher risk of experiencing depression, anxiety, and other mental disorders. This is not because of anything inherent in those identities, but because of how they are viewed and treated in society. When the culture that surrounds you is dangerous, discriminating, and cruel, you are bound to suffer emotionally. LGBTQ children know that society views them as different and not as worthy. They have a hard time envisioning their future because they don't see anyone like them in professional or even blue-collar jobs. They don't have role models and mentors to look up to. Because of this, they are more likely to engage in risky behaviors and to feel like their lives are not as valuable as others.

Discrimination against LGBTQ people exists almost everywhere there are humans, but it can be especially pronounced in conservative, religious communities.

Andrea Forsythe, an LGBTQ ally, posted the following on Instagram: "There are probably very few places more dangerous to the health of an LGBTQ youth or child than belonging to a conservative religious congregation. Even if the congregation is filled with loving people." Being kind doesn't make up for the hurtful doctrines of most Christian churches. When an LGBTQ youth is taught over and over that being gay is a sin and abhorrent to God, and that there are only two genders and anything else is immoral and wicked, the result is internalized homophobia, self-hatred, and the desire to leave the church, leave their family, and sometimes leave the world—through suicide.

When Brooke shared with us their second autobiography, I saw similarities between their experience and the patterns I had noticed in the stories I read on Instagram of LGBTQ kids growing up in religious homes. Brooke said they knew they were different by the time they were eleven or twelve. This is the most common age for LGBTQ individuals to realize their identity. Brooke also said they thought they would leave the house after graduating from high school and not be a part of our family anymore. Many of the youth in the other narratives had similar thoughts. They assumed their families wouldn't love them, wouldn't accept their identity, and wouldn't want them around. In truth, Bryan and I questioned—and even disagreed at times—with our church's standing on LGBTQ people over the years, but how was Brooke to know that? Brooke learned the church policies and teachings, and they saw us aligned with, and committed to, the church. The natural conclusion for them is that we agree with the church on LGBTQ issues.

Another theme running through these accounts was that if the youth had at least one person who supported them and believed in them, they fared better emotionally. I had read this statistic on an Instagram post, and I knew that it was true for Brooke. Their one person was Star (Gwen). I felt grateful to Star for being there for Brooke at their most trying time. Brooke knew they had at least one person to talk to about their identity and who could relate to them because they experienced the same thing.

I learned that when LGBTQ youth have families who accept and support them, they have lower rates of depression, anxiety, and suicide ideation. Thankfully, Bryan and I and the rest of the kids were able to be there for Brooke in that way. In the months following Brooke's coming out to us, I have had compliments from others on how well I handled the situation and how accepting I am of Brooke. I have asked myself, why did I have an easy time accepting their new identity? As I've contemplated this, I recognized three things. The first is my natural ability to be an under-reactor. I don't know how I achieved this, but the more extreme the situation, the calmer I am. When Brooke came out to me, I had had some warning from Kaitlin and time to adjust to the idea, and I knew this was a big deal, something that I needed to get used to right away—accept it and move on. The second reason is because of Brooke's innate lovable personality. As I have mentioned, they have always been sweet, mild-mannered, happy, and enthusiastic about life. It was their nature to be affectionate and loving, obedient, and a joy to be around. If they had been grumpy, rebellious, or hard to get along with, or if we'd had a history of arguing and contention, I might have been less willing to see them in a new light. I might have had defenses up that prohibited me from accepting Brooke however they were.

The third factor in my ease of accepting Brooke's identity is probably the most impactful. The work I had done with Liz in life coaching had prepared me to let go of one story and embrace a different one. I knew that my brain gets ideas about how the world *should* work or what my life *should* look like, and that sometimes holding on to those ideas can cause me pain. I have learned that you can choose to believe a new thought, even before your brain has a lot of reasons to accept it. In fact, one of my favorites of Liz's teachings was "believing things I don't have much evidence for makes me mentally stronger." That concept made sense to me, and I had worked to create a habit of identifying my stories and letting them go effortlessly. I was already in the process of releasing the Dream—the image of all our children staying in the church and conducting their lives like Bryan and I had. I could see that maintaining the impression that we would be happier like that only created heartache and caused me to miss out on the wonderful reality that was in front of me.

I applied this same logic to the theory of gender binary. I was fortunate to be able to quickly see that this was a construct our society had created. It was obvious to me that the idea that girls and boys must look and act a certain way, that there's nothing in between the two polarities, and that it's wrong to look or act differently than society's (or the church's) definitions were made-up beliefs. We could cling to them and continue to marginalize large groups of people who exist outside those norms, or we could see our notions for what they are: false paradigms that we had bought into.

I asked myself, what's wrong with changing? Why do we hold on to these outmoded opinions? It seemed to me there is no danger in letting these beliefs go, no harm to society. In fact, the opposite would happen, more members of our community could live happy, productive lives, free from discrimination and prejudice. Many of our constructs are based in fear, and I could see that they are nonsensical. Thankfully, most of secular society has accepted gay people and the concept of gay marriage. Now we have a new hurdle: recognizing and supporting transgender individuals and those with genders outside of the binary. These new and different ways of being feel scary because we're not used to them. But the sooner we can put down our defenses and embrace them, the happier we will be.

I am grateful to have LGBTQ children (Brooke as nonbinary and bisexual, and Kaitlin as bisexual), and I'm grateful that I was able to embrace them without qualms. It is a privilege to be their parent. I feel lucky to be able to be a part of the LGBTQ community. The people there are accepting and loving; they are a delight to be with. Brooke's coming out accelerated my ability to give up the Dream and focus on reality. Our family has learned so much through this experience. We've become more open and more sympathetic. We were able to get to know each other on a deeper level and love more unconditionally.

Of course, for religious people, it's not simply a matter of opening their minds to new ideas; this adjustment requires rejecting harmful church doctrines. This is not easy to do when you believe that your personal salvation requires a commitment to those doctrines. Maybe the first step is to acknowledge that LGBTQ individuals are as worthy of God's love and acceptance as anyone else and that any teachings that say otherwise are possibly wrong and definitely damaging and toxic. Another post I saw on Instagram said, "Being LGBTQ is like being left-handed. Some people are, most people aren't, and nobody really knows why. It's not right or wrong. It's just the way it is." This is an apt analogy because in centuries past, some religious leaders believed that being left-handed was of the devil. Left-handed children were forced to use their right hand and told to repent of whatever evil they had done to bring this curse upon themselves. It's easy to recognize that this idea is pernicious and false. Is it not possible that in the future, religious people will see the anti-LGBTQ doctrine in the same light?

There was another concept I had learned from coaching that helped me through this challenging time. Liz had taught me to ask the question, "How can I be the hero of this story and not the victim?" I returned to this query again and again, and the answers lifted and sustained me. It would be easy to think of myself as a victim, to ask "why me?" when faced with the mental health struggles of our family. But I liked to turn it around and ask, "why not me?" Who else could do it as well as me? I was made for this. I've got this. Thinking about how I'm the hero directs my brain toward reasons I am capable of handling this instead of focusing on how hard it is. I had knowledge and experience with mental health systems and treatments. I had Bryan to help navigate the doctors and medications. We had a strong foundation as a close, loving family. I remain calm in difficult situations and contemplate what I do and say before acting. Seeing myself as the hero of the story was comforting and motivating.

Thinking about the same situation in a new way created different feelings inside of me. This is the essence of cognitive therapy and life coaching: our feelings come from our thoughts. We tend to think that our circumstances create our emotions. We change things about our lives or ourselves to feel positive emotion. But, in truth, circumstances are neutral. They don't mean anything until we think a thought about them. All our feelings come from our thoughts. As Shakespeare wrote in *Hamlet*, "For there is nothing either good or bad, but thinking makes it so." When we know this, we are not subject to the whims and quirks of our circumstances. We regain control over our situations.

Changing our thoughts to create positive emotion is always an option, but it is not always easy to do. Often, we don't recognize that our thoughts create our emotions, and we essentially hand over the control of our emotions to our circumstances. Another barrier to shifting our thoughts is that our brain wants to hold onto its original idea, even though it's a painful one. With gentleness and curiosity, we can change our thoughts through a three-step process: become aware of your thoughts (all of them, even the ones you are afraid to admit you have); accept your thoughts (again, all of them—when you judge them, they go back into hiding); and allow the feelings they create (instead of resisting them). It's important not to rush this process. The brain thinks we need to hurry to get to positive emotion, but there's no reason to rush. Wherever we are, we are right on track.

I feel grateful for what I have learned from Liz and the peace it has brought to me. I used to think that feeling any negative emotion meant there was something wrong with me or my life. Before joining her program, I constantly compared my life to other people's and concluded that mine came up short. On one hand, I felt cheated and bitter that I didn't have what others had, but on the other hand, I felt guilty for being unhappy because I had so much.

Now I know that these thoughts and emotions are normal and expected. There's no getting rid of negative emotion. There's no offramp from that superhighway. There isn't a way of being or a way of living that prevents emotional pain. This is what it's like to be human; we may as well accept it. For example, our brain thinks it's useful to compare our lives to others to keep us safe and to make sure we have what we need. Once we understand this process, we can override these comparative thoughts and talk back to our brain. We can say, "Thanks for offering that, but I know that one way of living is not better than another; circumstances don't create our happiness, our thoughts about our circumstances do."

Our brain criticizes our thoughts and feelings to try to make us better. It says, "You shouldn't think that" or "You shouldn't feel that way." It thinks this is helpful and encouraging. Again, we can countermand those automatic thoughts with more conscious ideas. We can say, "Thanks for trying to help me improve, but it's okay that I have these self-pitying feelings. I'm human and they come sometimes." Learning how to respond to the critical thoughts my brain offers me is one of the greatest outcomes of working with Liz. I have replaced those self-deprecating notions with thoughts like, "You're not expected to be perfect," "Thanks for showing up today," and "I deserve love and forgiveness and grace." I learned to accept that I am fifty percent amazing and fifty percent a mess, and I love all of me.

Researcher Kristin Neff has studied this type of self-compassion and its advantages in our lives. She has become a leading advocate and expert on the subject. Her website says:

> Instead of mercilessly judging and criticizing yourself for various inadequacies or shortcomings, self-compassion means you are kind and understanding when confronted with personal failings—after all, who ever said you were supposed to be perfect?
>
> You may try to change in ways that allow you to be healthier and happier, but this is done because you care about yourself, not because you are worthless or unacceptable as you are. Perhaps most importantly, having compassion for yourself means that you honor and accept your humanness. Things will not always go the way you want them to. You will encounter frustrations, losses will occur, you will make mistakes, bump up against your limitations, fall short of your ideals. This is the human condition, a reality shared by all of us. The more you open your heart to this reality instead of constantly fighting against it, the more you will be able to feel compassion for yourself and all your fellow humans in the experience of life.[19]

We all fall victim to our internal censures and condemnations. It is a relief, however, to discover that we don't have to be at the mercy of the inner critic; experts like Neff and coaches like Liz can guide us to a gentler, more loving approach to ourselves and our perceived weaknesses.

If I hadn't known about the power of these important tools, I would have seen Brooke's mental health problems and LGBTQ identity as an indication of something wrong with me or something wrong with my life. Fortunately, I had done the work and learned how to manage my mind, so I was able to respond with peace and acceptance. Even though I was far from perfect at self-acceptance, I was better at it now than in the past. I had also improved at identifying my stories more quickly and loosening my grip on them. My past stories about how my children should be, the validity of a gender binary, or aspects of my personality that I disliked—these were made up and did not serve me. Letting go of them helped me appreciate and enjoy the reality of the present moment more fully.

CHAPTER 14

Moving On

Brooke's birthday came shortly after the new year. We gave them a calendar with astrological signs and information, a light that projected star patterns on the ceiling, and a sequin reversible Harry Styles pillow. Their favorite gift, however, was permission to dye their hair. They dyed it bright pink the day before their birthday. I was taken aback by the intensity of the color, but Brooke loved it. They went to day treatment on their birthday, and they put extra effort into their appearance: a black t-shirt with cartoon witches on it, a dark flannel over the shirt, black eyeliner and eyeshadow to create dark circles around their eyes, and a spiked choker necklace. All this mixed with the pink hair made quite a look. I had to mask my mild shock and discomfort because I wanted to support and accept Brooke however they chose to present themself. Brooke seemed elated, and their delight told me that this is who they really are and that they have wanted to exhibit their true self for some time.

Later in the day, I texted my mom and a few friends about Brooke's appearance. I included a picture I'd taken of them that morning and explained that I felt conflicted about this look. I wasn't used to this side of Brooke yet or this mode of expression. My friends were sympathetic and encouraging. My mom was living in New York City at the time. She said that this style is popular there and that she sees people with colored hair and Bohemian or goth style clothes every day. That comforted me. It's true that colored hair, piercings, and alternative interests (Tarot cards, crystals, astrology) were trending lately. When I talked to my friends, many of their kids were into the same things as Brooke. However, part of me felt like this isn't what a happy person looks like. I suspected that teens express this type of extreme appearance to cover up emotional pain and struggle. But maybe I had a different definition or perspective of "happy." Just because someone dresses differently than I do or is interested in ideas that seem foreign to me doesn't mean they are not content inside. Either way, I knew that with time, I would get used to Brooke's hair, makeup, and accessories.

In mid-January, a new term would begin at Brooke's regular high school. A few weeks prior, we had discussed with Brooke and their therapist, Jill, if this would be a good time for Brooke to go back to public school. Jill was pleased with Brooke's progress, and Brooke felt ready to go back. Around this time, their antidepressant medication started making a noticeable difference. Brooke had increased energy and more interest in activities. We continued to see steady improvement in their mood and overall functioning in the next few months. To ease the transition back to regular school, we worked with the counselor at the high school to lighten Brooke's schedule for the rest of the year. We replaced math and some AP classes with less intense classes like Office Aide and Adult Roles and Responsibilities.

Brooke's last time at day treatment was a cold and clear Friday in January. On the drive there, I noticed the mountains were white with snow, but only patches of dirty snow remained around the roads in the valley. Brooke was anxious to get the day over with and get back to high school the following Monday. When I picked them up at the end of the day, we both had to sign discharge papers, including a treatment plan. Part of the plan was twice a week therapy for Brooke with Lynn, the therapist I had emailed right after Brooke's suicide attempt. That turned out to be an excellent fit. Brooke felt a connection with Lynn and continued to improve under Lynn's care.

Even though this program hadn't been everything I'd hoped and dreamed, I was still thankful that we found it and that Brooke could attend. Brooke needed to have time pass without their grades suffering. The individual and group therapy were enough to get them past the crisis and onto a better path. As is often the case in these programs, Brooke met kids who had difficult life situations. Brooke felt sympathy for these other experiences and saw the advantages of their own life.

On January 18th, Brooke went back to high school and resumed their regular classes. Bryan and I watched in trepidation, hoping for a smooth transition. After a few weeks, however, we let out our breath and felt confident that Brooke would be all right. The new schedule kept Brooke busy but didn't overwhelm them. We still asked about their depression, anxiety, and desire to self-harm numbers two to three times a week. The numbers hung in the mid-range (between four and six) for quite a few months, but the desire to self-harm was low enough that we weren't alarmed for Brooke.

The construction of new homes on our street continued. Families moved into the finished homes, and in the warmer weather of spring, some of our neighbors completed their landscaping. The evolution from scraggly weeds and scattered rocks in the mud to green patches and trees in front of the houses was a welcome sight. It seemed life moved forward for our neighbors, as it did for us. We continued our Sunday family dinners with Kaitlin and Ben each week; Kaitlin neared graduation and Ben enjoyed his job. Bryan and I took turns getting up with Brooke and Sydney each morning to see them off to school. Their third term came to an end, and the fourth term began. Brooke got a job at a store in the mall that sold teenage paraphernalia such as t-shirts, body jewelry, and hair dye. They managed the balance of work and school with ease.

One hallmark of this time was my twice weekly phone conversations with Haley. For one of those calls, Kaitlin and Brooke (and sometimes Sydney) joined the chat. We knew that our goal was to cheer Haley, and we tried to find the balance between telling interesting stories from our lives and avoiding making her jealous and sad about missing out. It was a fine line, and at times the conversations got stale and slow. We'd end up playing with the filters, turning ourselves into witches and glowing suns. I worried frequently about our success (or lack thereof) in lifting Haley's spirits. Brooke complained after these conversations that they didn't know what to say to Haley and that they felt hesitant in supporting her on her religious mission.

Two fun events occurred in April: Sam took Brooke to the high school prom, and Kaitlin graduated from college. Brooke and Sam had been dating since late January. He was kind and adoring of Brooke, and Brooke liked him a lot, too. I loved seeing them together, going on fun dates and watching movies in the basement. I knew Sam was a great guy, and I was delighted to see Brooke being treated well and having fun.

Sam asked Brooke to prom with a pizza and a sign that said, "I know this is *cheesy*, but will you *chews* to go to prom with me?" Brooke found a prom dress online, and we had it altered by a local tailor. It turned out beautiful and fit them amazingly well. The dark navy satin fabric draped their body closely, and the dress had a long slit up the side. In the past, we would not have allowed our child to wear a dress like this because it had spaghetti straps and a low-cut back. Now we didn't have to be constrained by such rules, and it felt wonderful. It was a perfect dress for Brooke, and they loved wearing it.

Brooke and Sam joined with some other couples for their prom evening activities. Sam and the other boys planned dinner at a restaurant and a movie at his house after the dance. Bryan and I went to the high school for the promenade. It was fun to see the other couples, especially all the girls' dresses. Brooke and Sam looked stunning together. Sam is six-foot-five and wore a black and white checked suit with large flowers patterned up the legs and on one side of the jacket. The unusual suit drew a lot of attention. He had found it in a random shop on a recent trip back east with his family, and he had the confidence and charisma to pull it off. It was such a gratifying and enjoyable night.

For Kaitlin's graduation, the university did not hold in-person commencement ceremonies. They were still hesitant to get crowds together because of the Covid situation. Ben had graduated the year before, five weeks after the world shut down. The university didn't have time to prepare anything that year, but we held an at-home graduation, complete with speeches and diploma-awarding, that was almost as good. This year, however, the university knew they'd be doing graduation differently, and each college created a video with speakers and pictures of the graduates that families could stream anytime that day.

We watched the show and clapped for Kaitlin. Afterward, we went up to campus and took pictures of her in her cap and gown. It was a beautiful spring day, and we found many picturesque spaces with budding trees and colorful flowers. She graduated with honors in English. The thesis she'd told us about all year was finalized in early spring, and she had successfully defended it. Her goal is to become a professor, and she applied to many PhD programs but didn't get accepted. Some of them took fewer or no students because of Covid, and the number of applicants had greatly increased because of the economic downturn resulting from the pandemic. She did get accepted to a Masters in English program, however, at the same university she'd been attending. We were secretly glad because this meant she and Ben would live close to us for another year. I was confident she'd get into a PhD program on the next try and lamented the thought of them moving away.

Back in April of 2020, Bryan and I had planned a vacation to Las Vegas. We go there every year in late spring to enjoy the pool, wonderful restaurants, amazing shows, and fun shopping. Of course, we don't gamble or drink. Both those things were against our religion, and we don't have an interest in either of them, anyway. We had to cancel our trip, of course, when the world shut down in March of that year. We naïvely rescheduled for June but had to abandon those plans as well. A year later, in the spring of 2021, we heard things were opening in Vegas. We planned a trip for May, booked our hotel, and purchased tickets to two shows.

A few weeks before we were to leave, on Mother's Day evening, we found out that Haley was going to come home. She texted us that her mission president had decided it would be best for her mental health if she left her mission and got help at home. That was all the information we received that night. We didn't know when she'd fly home or why the sudden change. But Bryan and I both felt profound relief. Finally, this ordeal would be over. She could come home and receive professional care. We knew that was what she needed.

I found out more the next day when the mission president called me. He said that Haley had disclosed to his wife that she was self-harming. In her great distress, Haley had started scratching and cutting on her arms. The mission president explained that he now realized the seriousness of her condition and that she would be better off at home, getting specialized help. I knew Haley would be relieved that he made the decision for her. She didn't have to continue to wrestle with God for an answer or for confirmation of her choice.

She flew home that Thursday. I picked her up from the airport. It was six months from the time we had gone to that same location to drop her off for what we thought would be eighteen months of service. The airport was relatively empty, as it had been that day six months ago. Travel had not yet resumed to pre-Covid levels. I waited for her in the baggage claim area with a pit in my stomach. I didn't know what she would be like or what she was thinking or feeling. Finally, I saw her walking toward me, and I rushed to her. We embraced and she cried on my shoulder for a while. I wished for a peek into her psyche to see what thoughts were generating this emotion, but I didn't want to pepper her with questions right away. On the drive home she told me she felt relieved but also numb and disappointed and guilty. She needed time to adjust to regular life and to process the whole experience.

Some families in our religion would be devastated by this early return and view it as a failure. I obviously felt the opposite. I wasn't sad that she came home. I knew this was not only the right thing for her but also one more step toward my ability to stop participating in church. It had been challenging to support Haley on her mission while I wanted to separate from our church and from religion in general. Sometimes I would tell Haley on our calls about my frustrations with the church's LGBTQ policies or lack of acceptance of diverse people. After a few times of this, she asked me to stop, saying that those conversations made it harder to stay committed to the work. I refrained from discussing those things after that.

I was sad, however, that we were back in the same position of seeking the best solution for a child suffering from severe depression and anxiety. I directed my brain once again to thoughts about how I'm the hero and not the victim. We had been through this; we knew what to do. We had good health insurance, and I had the time to help Haley. By the time I picked her up at the airport, I had already set up appointments with doctors and therapists. It would once again be a waiting game, waiting for the medication to work and waiting for Haley to feel relief from her suffering. We knew now to keep the antidepressant pills and other medications locked up. At the ER crisis counselor's suggestion, I had purchased a lockbox from Amazon for this purpose. Each Sunday, I filled Haley and Brooke's weekly pill organizers and then put the bottles in the lock box. I held on to hope that Haley would see improvements eventually, as Brooke had.

With Haley's sudden return home, it looked like we would have to cancel our Vegas trip, again. Of course, we were willing to do so; taking care of Haley was more important than a leisure trip. It wasn't just that we wanted to have fun, though. Because of Covid and because of Brooke's needs, we hadn't been on a couple's trip for over a year, except for one night in a local hotel. Bryan and I loved to reconnect through traveling together; it had been an essential part of our marriage throughout the years. We had many fond memories of our previous times in Vegas and were anxious to recreate those, to relax and unwind. It had been an extremely difficult year, and we looked forward to rejuvenating our relationship by spending time alone.

We felt disappointed to cancel the trip but resigned to the fact. Then, a week after Haley returned, she got invited to go to Lake Powell with Amanda's family for ten days. Lake Powell is one of Haley's favorite places. She loves the water and enjoys wake surfing and knee boarding. She went with Amanda's family the previous year and had gotten to know her siblings and extended relatives. Haley particularly bonded with some of Amanda's young nieces and nephews. It would be a joy for her to see them again and feel their love. If there was one place that could boost Haley's spirits, it was on a houseboat in Lake Powell.

Once we knew her plans were secure, we rebooked our Vegas trip. We stayed at our favorite resort, the Bellagio. We love the conservatory and its awe-inspiring plant creations. They have lovely cafés and bistros with delicious food, and the pool is heavenly. It was designed to mimic Italian gardens with lush gardenia bushes and fragrant jasmine trellising the many wooden lattice arches. We were grateful that Brooke felt good enough to be on their own and that Haley would be watched over and well taken care of. I had spoken to Amanda's mom before Haley left. I told her about Haley's condition and that we'd be available if we needed to come pick her up or help in any other way.

The weather was beautiful in Vegas. It had been rainy and cold the weekend before, our original travel time, so we felt that the universe was working in our favor. One day we went to the Fashion Show mall, one of our Vegas favorites. Although many of the stores there were also in our city, the Vegas stores seemed to have a better selection, and we always found cute new clothes. After looking around for a while, we ate lunch at a Mexican restaurant connected to the mall. We sat on the outdoor patio in the sun.

After we ordered our food, we started discussing our feelings about the church. We needed an update to our ongoing conversation on this topic and had decided that our trip to Vegas would be a good time to do that.

"Where should we begin?" I ventured.

"Tell me where you're at, especially since Haley came home," Bryan said.

"I feel more ready to leave than ever. I'm relieved that Haley came home because she needed help, but I'm also relieved because I don't have to pretend to be supportive of her mission any longer. I'm not quite ready to announce my intentions to the kids, though. I want to give Haley time to acclimate to normal life, and I want to assess her commitment to religion. I don't want to throw her off balance any more than she already is by making this big change. I can wait for her sake, but I look forward to being my more authentic self."

"Okay, that makes sense. What will you say to people when you leave? People will want to know your reasons." The waiter brought our food and set it before us. Bryan started eating while I talked.

I spoke enthusiastically, "I have rehearsed this in my head many times. I have my list of about thirteen what I call 'Factors'—things I have come to understand and believe that led me away from Christianity. I want people to know the causes of my disillusionment, all the disputes I have with the doctrine." I had described the factors to Bryan one day a few months ago. I'd been working on the list for about a year, adding items when they came to me. The factors included the ideas about each group believing they were special, white supremacy being tied to Christianity, and the final judgment being illogical, as well as the more personal aspects, such as wanting to feel approval of my adult children and disliking the guilt-inducing "shoulds" of the church.

Bryan looked slightly dismayed. "It seems easier to say it's because Brooke is LGBTQ. People can understand that."

"That feels disingenuous to me," I countered. "If I say that, people will assume I am upset about their identity. They will think that I still believe the doctrine and want to stay but can't because of this one issue: needing to support Brooke. That is not accurate. I'm not troubled by Brooke's identity. I'm thankful to have a child like this who helped me see the wider world and accept people who are different from me. I wouldn't change Brooke in the slightest. And I want people to know that. This requires explaining that I've lost faith in Christian doctrines in general, *and* that I don't want to support the homophobic practices of our church anymore."

The waiter stopped by to bring Bryan another Diet Coke. I took a bite of my food and looked at him. He seemed conflicted. "Does that bother you?" I asked.

"No, not at all. That makes sense, and I support whatever you want to say to people. I'm not sure I'm ready to leave though. I want to be on the same page as you because we are always in sync."

We smiled at each other over this. It is remarkable how similar and compatible we have been throughout the years. We almost always agree or are easily able to see the other person's side. Our love is so strong; it is like an invisible cord binding us together. That cord gets thicker and stronger with every deep conversation, every time Bryan makes me laugh so hard my eyes water, and all the intimate interactions between us each day. When we're in the same room, I feel pulled toward him and want to be next to him. When he's gone at work, I want to tell him my thoughts and accomplishments throughout the day.

Bryan continued, "I like it when we are united, but on the other hand, I don't want to leave simply because you are, you know? I want it to be my own decision."

"I can understand that," I agreed. "What are the pros and cons in your mind?"

"I agree with most of your 'factors,' and I struggle to support a church that leaves LGBTQ people out of heaven. However, I feel like my commitment to the church has brought many blessings into my life. For example, in my undergraduate studies and throughout medical school, I prayed before every test. I believe I was heard and received divine help. I attribute my success in becoming a physician with my religious beliefs and my strict adherence to those principles. In addition, being in the church brought us together, and you are the greatest thing in my life. My devotion to the teachings of the church and my relationship with God have helped me be a better parent and more patient with our kids. And I think that my success in this new practice is due in part to my involvement with the church. It seems ungrateful to leave the church when it has brought me so much.

"My home was kind of chaotic growing up. After my parents got divorced, we didn't go to church for a while. That was a difficult time, for many reasons. Then my mom got remarried, we moved, and we attended church again and became active in our congregation. A lot of great things happened for me at that time—I had a fun group of friends, I did well in school, I became a lifeguard and swim instructor and had a large income for a teenager. It's hard not to attribute that success to our participation in the church."

I was moved by his explanation. I knew these stories of his background, but I hadn't put together the correlation with church activity. I could see his point of view and felt sympathetic to his reasons. I wanted to point out an alternate version, however, for him to consider.

I said, "Maybe those good things came to you because of who you are and what you did. Maybe you brought them to yourself through your hard work and good attitude. It's possible that there didn't need to be a God or a religion involved and you could have done all that on your own. I know it's helpful to believe in something and feel like you'll be guided and assisted, but you can leave the church and still believe in a power in the universe that we can tap into for help or comfort. I don't think that has to go away."

"That's true," Bryan responded. "I'll have to think more about that. I have another worry in the back of my mind. It is that if I leave the church, my colleagues and patients will think less of me. That might impact the success of our practice. I feel compelled to do what I can to make the practice thrive, not only for me but also for my partners."

"Yeah," I nodded, "I can see how you would think that. But do you really think patients would change doctors if you weren't in the church? How many would actually do that, and would it make that big of an impact?"

"Who knows?" Bryan said. We were done eating by this point and the waiter brought the bill and cleared the dishes. Bryan continued, "I'm glad we are having this conversation because I've been thinking about all this for a while and wanted to review it with you when we had the time. It's always helpful to talk through things together."

I nodded and held his hand across the table. He continued, "I know this may be prideful, but I like being an upstanding member of the community. I like serving as president of the men's group and helping the congregation. I like making my mom proud. I know she is pleased with all my successes: being a doctor, having a great family and raising them in the church, and serving in leadership positions in the church. Those things bring her a lot of joy. I worry that I would disappoint her and others in my family if I left."

"I know," I agreed. "That is hard. Those thoughts are natural. It's nice to be the successful one. But our kids aren't going to live up to your mom's expectations of being committed to the church anyway. And it's okay to change your mind, to expand your perspective and see things in a new way."

We sat in silence for a moment, lost in our own thoughts.

I spoke again, "It can be confusing. When you're in the leadership meetings, and everyone is trying to help others and create a loving feeling in the congregation, you feel like the church has a bright glow and is full of goodness. It's like there are two sides to the church, and it's easy to face the light side, to focus on how it has helped you and others to flourish in life. That experience is real. Being part of a religious congregation has many benefits.

"But there is a dark side, too. Your back is facing that right now, and it's not pleasant to turn around and examine it. The dark side contains the people who feel marginalized and not included in the doctrine. It also encompasses the judgment and exclusion of certain people and those who never feel like they live up to the expectations and requirements of the church. There's a lot of harm created in religious communities. The prohibition of LGBTQ members from full church involvement is just one example of that."

"It's true," Bryan said. "And now that we've seen more of that dark side, it's hard to unsee it."

We were silent again, pondering this realization. It was time to sum up the conversation and leave the restaurant.

"Well, you don't have to decide today," I began. "I am glad to hear your thoughts and understand where you're coming from. I'm fine with you continuing to go. That doesn't bother me. Take your time and do what you feel is best. We should check in with each other occasionally. But I am ready to let go of a lot of things: my vision of our family's future in the church, our expectations of our kids' behaviors and beliefs, my narrow views on sexual and gender identities, and my involvement in the church."

"Ok, that's good to know," Bryan said. "I appreciate your support. This can be hard on couples—when one spouse leaves the church and the other stays. But I want you to know that I'm okay with your leaving. You are on your own journey, and it's not my place to judge that or prevent you from doing what you feel is right. I have no reason to judge because I don't feel strongly that everyone needs to be religious. I am not worried about heaven or hell or what will happen in the eternities; I know it will work out. If there is a way for us to be together after we die, we will find it. We are meant for each other."

We both smiled, and Bryan squeezed my hand. I already knew that he wasn't upset that I was leaving, but it was nice to hear him say it. Some spouses in his position might feel frustrated and think, "This isn't what I signed up for," because when we met and married, we were both committed to the church. It's common to hold your spouse to an old expectation and try to stifle any shift in beliefs or personality. Luckily, Bryan and I respected and loved each other enough to let the other person change and grow and be who they wanted to be. Our marriage had always been a source of comfort and strength for us, and this new dynamic didn't change that.

CHAPTER 15

If You Leave, Where Will You Go?

In their book *Living Deeply: The Art & Science of Transformation in Everyday Life*, authors Marilyn Schlitz, Cassandra Vieten, and Tina Amorok define consciousness transformations as "profound internal shifts that result in long-lasting changes in the way you experience and relate to yourself, others, and the world." They further explain that this "change in [your] perception of reality" allows you to discover more fully who you are and the true nature of the world, "independent of the social expectations and cultural conditioning that had previously shaped [your] sense of self."[20]

In the past year, I feel that my consciousness has been transformed. When I read this definition in *Living Deeply*, it described my recent experience perfectly. My perception of reality has been altered, I have a better understanding of the nature of the world, and I have changed the way I relate to myself and others. "Profound internal shift" is an accurate description. Learning about, and working with, life coaching laid the groundwork for this change. Having Brooke come out as LGBTQ gave me the permission I needed to fully embrace these new beliefs and do what my conscience was telling me to do: leave Christianity.

I knew if I stopped participating in the church, others would ask, "If you leave, where will you go?" Humans tend to see things in black and white, and I know that many Christians think if you do not believe in Christ, you don't believe in anything, and subsequently, you are immoral and wicked. The members of my church are taught that if you renounce the church, there is no other path that will bring happiness; you are doomed to misery. If congregants leave and then struggle with substance use, relationships, or employment, active members see this as a consequence of disobeying commandments. They don't recognize that these difficulties might stem from being ostracized from family and community or from residual guilt arising from indoctrinated ideas.

As I contemplated parting with Christianity, I asked myself, "If I don't believe in this, what do I believe?" As a baseline, I knew that there was a power in ourselves and in the universe that we can tap into for help in making decisions, obtaining guidance, and feeling comfort. Forsaking organized religion did not mean I had to give up access to that potential. Even when I assumed that God or the Holy Spirit helped me in these ways, I imagined that God had created our minds and bodies such that they would generate certain thoughts and feelings when we focused on Him. I believed He built a mechanism into our brain that produced a desired result when we had certain convictions and actions.

For example, the religious habits of prayer and daily scripture study bring benefits such as inner peace and improved relationship skills. I was taught that this is because God blesses you when you spend time speaking to Him and reading His words. But research shows that these same benefits can be attained through gratitude and meditation practices, which don't require any religious principles.

Prayer is, at its essence, a gratitude practice; listing blessings from God directs the mind toward the good things in our lives. Scripture study has parallels to meditation. In both, you shut out the external world and focus on something for a prescribed length of time. As you try to get still, thoughts of your to-do list or previous conversations crowd your mind. Concentrating on the archaic language of the King James version of the Bible is challenging. Meditation requires the same stillness and concentration, and produces the same benefits—enhanced self-awareness, lengthened attention span, and improved emotional health, to name a few.

My habits of prayer and scripture reading helped me not because God blessed me, but because they utilized mechanisms intrinsic to the human brain. The specific religious values I attached to these practices were unnecessary to access the gains.

However, being part of a religious community does aid your belief in the power of the mind. I hardly went a week without hearing a story of how God intervened to bless someone's life (in other words, how that person harnessed the power of their mind by visualizing a God who would help them). In church meetings, magazines, and lessons, and in regular conversations with friends, I heard faith-promoting stories about God sending blessings or aid.

For example, at the end of the month, someone with little money struggles with whether to pay their tithes to the church or pay their rent. They worry and pray and finally decide to have faith and pay tithes first. Shortly after, they receive an unexpected paycheck, a bonus, or an anonymous donation that covered the rent. God provided! Less dramatic instances involve the person knowing the right thing to say to a worried friend, feeling prompted to help someone in a certain way, or being led to a book or website to get help with a parenting problem. Many people shared these stories of divine help, and I knew them to be valid.

These occurrences may seem fantastical to a non-religious person, but they are commonplace for members of my church. How do you explain this if you don't attribute these favors to God or the Holy Spirit? Answer: that person harnessed the power of their mind by visualizing a God who would help them. Focusing on the thing we want and trusting we will receive it greatly increases the chances that it will happen. But whether we hold religious views or not, we can create these experiences for ourselves.

Granted, religion has a lot of tools that are useful for generating these mystical experiences. The imperative to maintain certain habits (like reading scriptures and praying), the community of followers encouraging each other, and the directive to always have faith combine to create the perfect landscape in the human mind for believing that you can attain your desired outcome. Things don't always go as the religious person wants them to, of course, but these small "miracles" happen with enough frequency to keep the flame of faith alive. Expecting these types of things to happen makes them more likely to occur and sharpens the mind to look out for them.

This remarkable power is available to everyone, however. Its benefits are not limited to religious people. Throughout the years, as I read books and articles and listened to stories of people outside of religion, I found that people from all walks of life have these types of experiences. People felt nudged into some action or drawn to a particular profession. Others had serendipitous events occur that couldn't be explained by chance alone. People even heard voices of warning or saw visions of deceased loved ones coming to comfort them. Cultures that are vastly different from Christianity have beliefs about ancestors watching over them or one or many gods whom they can solicit for help. But even people who have no such culture and no acceptance of the metaphysical occasionally feel that something unexplainable has happened.

There is a term for these experiences: noetic. It comes from the Greek adjective *noētikos*, meaning intellectual, and from the verb *noein*, meaning to think. It has been used since the 1600s, but in 1902 the philosopher William James defined it further as "states of insight into depths of truth unplumbed by the discursive intellect. They are illuminations, revelations, full of significance and importance, all inarticulate though they remain; and as a rule, they carry with them a curious sense of authority..."[21]

In 1973, the astronaut Edgar Mitchell cofounded The Institute of Noetic Sciences (IONS) after he had this type of insight as he stared at Earth from the window of his space capsule. In that moment, his consciousness was transformed, and he "realized that the story of ourselves as told by science—our cosmology, our religion—was incomplete and likely flawed." He experienced a profound sense of universal connectedness which helped him "recognize that the Newtonian idea of separate, independent, discrete things in the universe wasn't a fully accurate description. [We] needed...a new story of who we are and what we are capable of becoming."[22]

He created the Institute to discuss his experience, hear similar stories from others, and study how beliefs, thoughts, and intentions affect the physical world. IONS seeks to reveal the interconnected nature of reality through scientific exploration and personal discovery.[23]

In a 2009 article entitled "What Are Noetic Sciences?", Cassandra Vieten, the then-president and CEO of IONS (and one of the authors of *Living Deeply*), explained that the noetic sciences use a multidisciplinary approach to "bring objective scientific tools and techniques together with subjective inner knowing to study the full range of human experience."[24] Traditional science relies solely on external observation and objective evaluation and measurement. But other ways of knowing—subjective feelings, such as hunches or intuition—can't be explained or proven but are nonetheless real. Organized religions have long accepted these experiences and attributed them to God or the Spirit. The noetic sciences seek to bring these opportunities to everyone, regardless of adherence to religious behaviors and dogma.

In her article, Vieten affirms, "Noetic experiences are real, they influence our health, our behaviors, and our lives, and they provide important clues about who and what we are and what we may be capable of. So real-life noetic scientists are dedicated to their rigorous exploration and to the potential that [they] hold for human evolution."[25]

The tendency to see beyond yourself or have an expansive feeling is the basis of religious involvement but isn't limited to religious people. People everywhere, of all religions and no religion, experience these same mystical phenomena. The key is confidence that they can and will happen to you. Noetic experiences happen regularly and increase in frequency as you expand your consciousness and improve your ability to see and experience them. It is true that it takes "faith"—it just doesn't have to be faith in any certain religion.

Because of my experiences with my religion, however, I had more of a tendency to believe in the possibility of noetic experiences and help from "the universe." As I learned about the wider world and saw that these experiences weren't limited to religious people, I expanded my perspective. I deduced that the noetic experiences weren't coming from God, but from the power of the mind.

Working with Liz in her coaching program strengthened my understanding of noetic experiences and led me to see their more comprehensive and unhindered availability. I learned how our feelings come from thoughts, not from external circumstances. Those feelings fuel our action, and the actions determine our results. This means that if we choose to espouse an idea, a certain result will follow. Sometimes it can seem like magic, but this is how our brains and our bodies are designed, whether by an omnipotent creator or by chance of chemical interactions is irrelevant. Liz taught me that you can choose to believe a thought even if your brain doesn't have evidence for it. This sounds suspiciously like hoping for a miracle. What is a miracle if not something that occurs in the absence of compelling evidence that it should happen? This is also known as the law of attraction, the idea that the universe will respond to the thoughts and energies you put out into the world. When we trust in something, our brain creates that thing.

As I try to define what I believe now, it comes down to this: I believe in the noetic sciences. I think there is a power in thoughts that we don't yet understand. I am confident that thoughts not only affect how we feel and act and therefore the results we get, but they literally attract things into our lives—people, job offers, car accidents, parking places, trips, money. Our thoughts send out tentacles of energy that interact with people and animals and even inanimate objects. I don't know how it works, but I'm convinced there's something there, an unseen force that is more powerful than any of us know. I believe we can best access this power in the universe and inside us when we are in alignment with our best selves. Getting in alignment is a process of practicing gratitude, accepting reality, allowing emotions, and becoming aware of our thoughts and feelings and how they create our results. It takes knowledge and practice to get better at staying in alignment, but this skill can be learned and strengthened.

I feel slightly sheepish stating these views. These are concepts that can't yet be proven or fully explained. But that doesn't mean they never will be. Electricity is an invisible force that existed even before we learned about how it works and harnessed its potential. It's possible that there are sources of energy we haven't discovered. As scientists delve into the very small (subatomic particles) and the very large (the cosmos), they find unexpected and sometimes unexplainable things happening. Quantum physics, dark matter—these are concepts that sound like science fiction and yet they're not.

It is short-sighted to dismiss these ideas simply because we don't understand them. Any sufficiently advanced technology is indistinguishable from magic. The experiences of religious people are real. They come about because of the power of the mind. When we believe in something, our brain creates that thing. This is an underused power by most people, but members of my faith utilize it often. Watching that process and experiencing it for myself convinced me of its veracity.

I may sound crazy, but I am in good company. Nikola Tesla, a genius inventor and electrical engineer from the early 1900s, known for his contributions to our modern electricity supply system, said, "The day science begins to study non-physical phenomena, it will make more progress in one decade than in all the previous centuries of its existence."[26]

Furthermore, studies from the burgeoning field of positive psychology have proven again and again the power of the mind. In the 1990s, pioneering psychologists such as Martin Seligman and Tal Ben-Shahar decided to switch from the usual study of emotional suffering and mental problems to investigating what factors bring happiness and success. The results from research in this new field surprised them.

Experiments repeatedly demonstrated that the mind creates what it believes to be true and that our emotional state has a significant effect on our outcomes and success.

A student of Seligman's, Shawn Achor, wrote *The Happiness Advantage*, condensing into one awe-inspiring book the findings from decades of this research. I read this book in amazement. Here was scientific research backing the concepts I'd learned in life coaching. These principles have been tested in rigorous, double-blind, and peer-reviewed experiments and found to be sound. The book has seemingly endless examples of the power of the mind. Tweaking the mindset of study participants changed their results. Telling them to expect something made that thing come true more often. Experiencing different emotions changed their ability to observe and process information. The mental and emotional state of the mind proved to be incredibly important.

For example, experts had concluded in the 1950s that it was physically impossible for a human to run a mile in less than four minutes. But in 1954, Roger Bannister did it in 3 minutes 59.4 seconds. Once this imaginary barrier was broken, runners everywhere beat that four-minute mark. Why the change? Runners now trusted it could be done.[27]

Believing something can happen is powerful, as is working at a task while feeling positive emotions. Our brains are hardwired to perform at their best when they are in a confident frame of mind. Studies have shown that when in a positive mood (as opposed to a neutral state), salespeople sell fifty-six times more, doctors make diagnoses with almost three times more intelligence and creativity, and students perform better on math tests.[28]

Positive emotions expand our ability to problem solve and come up with creative solutions. Negative emotions do the opposite. Our vision and range of actions are narrowed when we are stressed, angry, or sad. This is partly because happiness neurotransmitters like dopamine and serotonin engage our brain's higher levels of learning. In that state, we can "organize new information, keep that information in the brain longer, and retrieve it faster later on."[29] Without those chemicals in our brain, we are less capable of quick and creative thinking and complex analysis of problems.

In another example of the power of the mind, Ellen Langer conducted an experiment in 1979 that had dramatic results. A group of seventy-five-year-old men spent a week at a retreat center pretending it was the year 1959 and that they were fifty-five years old. They dressed and acted like they did at that time, including discussing President Eisenhower and other political and personal events from those years. The conversations and the environment were designed to make the participants see the world through the lens of being fifty-five. Before and after the retreat, the men were tested on physical aspects associated with aging: strength, posture, memory, and cognition. At the end of the week most of them had progressed in every category. Their eyesight improved, they were more flexible, and they had better hand strength. Surprisingly, even their physical appearances changed. When asked to guess the ages of the men in pictures before and after the experiment, random people said they looked on average three years younger than when they arrived.

This remarkable study showed that the mind creates what it believes to be true. The way we perceive ourselves has a direct influence on the physical aging process. Our external "reality" is far more malleable than many of us think, and far more dependent on the eyes through which we view it.[30]

The Happiness Advantage also describes multiple studies that demonstrate the placebo effect, an occurrence so common we take it for granted. But how is it possible that patients given a sugar pill still get the result attributed to the medication? When a person is told something will happen, his mind somehow creates that experience. Participants in a Japanese study were blindfolded and told their right arms were being rubbed with a poison ivy plant. Within a few hours, all thirteen of the students' arms had itching sores and redness—even though the plant used was not poison ivy but a harmless shrub.[31]

In another experiment, the cleaning staff of seven different hotels were divided into two groups. Researchers told half of the employees that their cleaning work was beneficial exercise, for example, vacuuming is a cardio workout. The other half were not told anything. Several weeks later the two groups were tested. Those primed to see their work as exercise had multiple objective measurements of improved health, including pounds lost and cholesterol numbers decreased.[32]

This happened so often in these experiments that psychologists created a term for it: expectancy theory. The human brain is structured to act on what our brain expects will happen next. The brain patterns these expectations create can be as genuine as those created by real events. The same complex set of neurons fire together when we anticipate an event as when it actually takes place.

In the book, Achor emphasized, "[This] point is so important, it bears repeating: *The mental construction of our daily activities, more than the activity itself, defines our reality.*"[33] This is precisely the doctrine of life coaching. When you believe something will happen, your brain will get to work making it happen. Your thoughts create feelings, which lead to actions that create your result. Priming yourself to expect a favorable outcome instructs your brain to recognize the outcome more readily when it is within your reach. When you stay in positive emotion, you have a better outcome because you can think more clearly, problem-solve more effectively, and see more options. This relates to the coaching principle of accepting reality. Drop the part where you're mad and frustrated that the event happened, and you can stay in positive emotion to deal with the outcomes more successfully.

A video created for a study on attention and perceptions shows about ten people playing basketball, half in white jerseys and half in black.[34] Participants were instructed to count the number of times the white team passes the ball. At the end of the video, they were asked, "Did you see the large gorilla walk through the players, pause in the middle, and look at the camera?" People in the study thought the researchers were crazy. There was no gorilla. They would not accept that a gorilla (more specifically, a man in a gorilla suit) was there until they saw the video again. Sure enough, he walked through the game and paused to look at the camera. How could they have missed it?! The answer is that they instructed their brains to look for one thing (white-shirted team members passing the ball), and their field of vision narrowed such that it could not absorb other sensory input.

The practical applications of this limitation of our brain are numerous and include opinions on race, social status, LGBTQ identities, and the outcomes of adhering to a religious faith. We have beliefs and stories that we've picked up from our families and social media. When we hold tightly to these ideas, we scan for verification of them, which hinders our ability to see other people's experiences clearly. If you are convinced the world fairly rewards hard work, then you will see lack of success as a failure to exert enough effort, and you will be less able to see the social structures (such as racial inequality) that block some people's advancement. If you suppose that following certain rules is the only way to happiness, then your brain will filter out information that doesn't conform with that thought and highlight examples that do.

We think we see all of reality, but we don't. We see the world in a narrow way, with colored perspectives and obstacles in our view. These impediments block a full and comprehensive experience of existence. If we allow ourselves to consider new information as it comes in, we can peel back the stories we are attached to and see things in a new way.

It can be challenging to open your mind to new information. Some people feel that if they revise their values, it means what they did before was wrong. Again, life coaching had taught me that this is just a story. Our brain sometimes wants to sell us on defining our past behaviors as mistakes, but we don't have to attach to that idea. The universe is always conspiring in our favor, and we are always operating to the best of our abilities. Having faith in those two concepts means nothing has gone wrong in the past, and there is nothing to fear in the future. Adopting those tenets brings great comfort.

Another barrier to flexibility in beliefs is the realization that if you accept new facts and change your worldview, then you might not fit in with your existing groups, such as family, friends, political parties, or colleagues. This is what the authors of *Living Deeply* refer to as "the social expectations and cultural conditioning that had previously shaped [your] sense of self."[35] Sometimes, social stakes can be so high that it feels impossible to change our minds. Maybe I had less rigidity in my viewpoints because I don't entirely belong to any one group. I have dueling identities: intellectual versus spiritual. I have always thought differently from my orthodox friends at church, and I didn't entirely fit in with my liberal, non-religious family members. There's no large group of family or friends from whom I feel pressure to be one way or the other. I've always navigated both.

Allowing elasticity in your beliefs is necessary to be able to develop your mind and grow as new evidence comes in. Part of adult human development is to update your models and worldviews. This is what happened to me over the past year—new evidence came in about my family, their struggles, their LGBTQ identities, their feelings about the church, and the effect of the church's policies and doctrines on LGBTQ youth. I allowed this information to sink in. I contemplated it and compared it to my existing thoughts and decided something needed to change. My consciousness transformation led me to understand that there's no need to fear how we or others act or live. We can love and accept everyone. I realized there's no need for the strict rules I had been adhering to, especially when those rules isolate us or others. After my change in perspective, I saw the world in a more open and generous light, and I felt more connected with others and the universe. In short, this way of relating to the world felt better.

Part of my consciousness transformation was recognizing the difference between religion and spirituality. I've heard it said that the former has answers you can't question, and the latter has questions you can't answer. Orthodox members of my church often say they're glad they have the truth (the answers) and know how the world and the eternities work. But that unyielding belief blocks new ideas. Novel thoughts are dangerous in my religious community. Members are warned to stay away from certain information that might detract from their faith.

It can be unpleasant to have unanswerable questions, but it can also bring greater enlightenment. When you're comfortable with ambiguity, life becomes fuller, more possibilities present themselves, and there are greater opportunities for joy. Life is more complex and layered than we often recognize. Seeing the world in a dogmatic way simplifies things, but it doesn't allow for the three-dimensionality of life.

The Austrian poet Rainer Maria Rilke said,

> Have patience with everything that remains unsolved in your heart. Try to love the questions themselves, like locked rooms and like books written in a foreign language. Do not now look for the answers. They cannot now be given to you because you could not live them. It is a question of experiencing everything. At present you need to live the question. Perhaps you

> will gradually, without even noticing it, find yourself experiencing the answer, some distant day.[36]

I am okay living in the question for now. I think of it as making room for the magic. I don't know all things, and that's okay.

Religion contains rules, ceremonies, and rituals developed by man to create conformity and uniformity in the approach to God.[37] The emphasis is on the institution. Religion asks, "What practices, rites, or rituals should I follow? What is right and wrong? What is true or false?" Spirituality, on the other hand, is discovered individually and leads people to ask, "Where do I find meaning? How do I feel connected? How should I live?" Morality is doing what is right, regardless of what you are told; religion is doing what you are told, regardless of what is right.

I see this tension between what you are told and what is right in families in my church who have an LGBTQ family member. They often feel betrayed by the teachings of the church, which say that their LGBTQ loved one is sinful and can't be with them in heaven. They know in their hearts this isn't right. They know their child or sibling is a good person, a regular person who wants the same things everyone else wants, not an immoral or deviant person. And yet they also feel a commitment to their religious beliefs. It can be difficult to know what to do and who to listen to.

Another reason I moved toward spirituality is because of its focus on the wisdom and power that comes from internal sources as opposed to knowledge and redemption coming from external sources. Religion's dualistic paradigms (good/

evil, heaven/hell) generate narrow-mindedness and intolerance. Spirituality encourages oneness paradigms; there's no us versus them. We are all one. The freedom of choice about behavior and appearance in spirituality is in stark contrast to high-demand religions, where everyone must be the same, follow the same journey, and have the same opinions. Any deviation from that is viewed with suspicion. I love that spirituality teaches that every person has their own unique path and journey; differences are okay. That feels satisfying to me.

My definition of spirituality considers how you relate to something bigger than yourself and how you find meaning in life. There is a lot of room for diversity in how you search for these things and the way you accomplish them. There is no one right way. Spirituality to me means having faith that you'll be guided continually to new sources of truth and wisdom. Spiritual people are not godless, they honor the god in all of us. This is how I want to live.

Religion teaches that growth and change come from self-recrimination, guilt, and shame. There's no assessment of personal desires but a subjugation of your own will to do what is prescribed. Self-sacrifice, duty, and pity for others are the focus. Spirituality, on the other hand, permits you to consider what you want to do and why and how to accomplish that. The focus is on the joy, bliss, spontaneity, and compassion within your being. This is one of Liz's main teachings: we think that allowing ourselves to do what we want and giving ourselves grace and acceptance (as opposed to having rigid rules of behavior and guilt and shame for shortcomings) will lead to selfishness and laziness, but it is the opposite. When we give ourselves a choice, let go of "shoulds," and have unbounded self-compassion, we will seek after meaningful, helpful, fulfilling behaviors. This still requires our hard work and sacrifice, but we do it from a different motivation.

As part of my spirituality, I believe strongly that our lives are interwoven with every other person and with all species. We have an underlying unity and connection. This is almost antithetical to the Christian religion. Christianity says because of our membership in this religious community, we are the *only ones*, we're better, we have the knowledge. In this sentiment, there's a lack of humility, a lack of desire to learn from others, and no acknowledgement of our need for others, especially if they are unlike ourselves.

Identifying these differences cleared my vision and helped me see the path forward. I want to consider new information, to hold questions in my heart when the answers don't come easily. I want to feel connected to other people and the universe and find meaning in life through my work and my interactions with others. I am ready to allow myself and others to be on their own unique path, to let go of judgment and condemnation, and to feel love, acceptance, and compassion as often as possible.

Observing my own and others' noetic experiences, learning about the power of the mind in life coaching and from positive psychology research, and being willing to let go of the dogmatic teachings of my religion have led to my consciousness transformation. I'm thankful that I had enough flexibility of belief to release old ideas and allow fresh ones to sink in. I appreciate my new, more expansive view of the world and the opportunity to discover more fully who I am as I live more authentically. I know this profound internal shift will be long-lasting.

CHAPTER 16

"The Rules Get Fewer and the Swimsuits Get Smaller!"

In June, Sydney turned fourteen. During the events of the past year, she had mostly been a spectator. She knew what was happening with Brooke; she watched us worry about them and coordinate their mental health care. I tried to stay conscious of Sydney's needs though. I knew that sometimes parents get caught up in the drama of one child, and the other one gets ignored. I checked in with her occasionally, but she usually didn't have much to say. In December, after Brooke got home from their inpatient care, I set up a counselor for Sydney to see. She was compliant about going, but she didn't love it.

After about five sessions, I could see she wasn't connecting with her therapist, so we discontinued her therapy.

We were more open as a family now, and I knew that would be an advantage for Sydney as she went through her adolescence. We talked about our medications and our therapists and updated each other on our mental health journeys. Once a month, we held formal mental health check-in meetings. In these meetings, Bryan and I talked about the positives and negatives in our lives. Sydney was reticent and declined to say anything. Brooke, on the other hand, was forthright in talking about their therapy, what was going well and what bothered them. They were a good example to Sydney, even if Sydney wasn't ready to share her thoughts and feelings.

I joked with Sydney that all the siblings have had a mental health crisis in their junior year. "So, let me know when it's coming!" I teased. But I was partly sincere. Now I expected these challenges and wanted her to know it was okay to talk to me if her mental health declined. I no longer saw these situations as a failure of my parenting or our family dynamics. I knew that they just were, and we could resist them or embrace them as part of the human experience, as one of the many cards you can be dealt in life. I hoped that by taking this perspective, I could ease the stress or pressure on her.

Bryan worried about Sydney in another way. He wanted to give her the same experience that we'd provided the other children, namely, teaching them about the gospel in case they want to embrace it one day. He was troubled by the idea that if we didn't have family scripture study and prayer and go to church as a family, we denied her that opportunity. I didn't see things the same way. First, she had little desire to go to church right now. Most teenagers think church and church activities are boring, and she was no different. Second, from my new perspective, I saw that raising children in the church can do as much harm as it can good. If we let her finish her teen years with fewer rules and restrictions, maybe she will have less guilt, anxiety, and depression in the long run. Bryan asked her each week if she wanted to go with him to church. Most of the time she said no, but occasionally she went.

By coincidence, the Pride march in our area was on the same day as Sydney's birthday, which was a Sunday. In the past, I would have wanted to go to church on a Sunday and keep the Sabbath day holy by not shopping or doing anything recreational. Pride events certainly didn't fit the criteria for appropriate Sabbath day activities, according to my religion. But this was a new year and a new me, and I wanted to be involved with, and supportive of, any LGBTQ-affirming activities.

Bryan was out of town, but the rest of the kids came with me. Kaitlin and Ben made the hour-long drive to the capitol building separately, as did Haley and Amanda. Brooke and Sydney came in my car. The kids were mildly surprised that I would skip church for this event, but they were more enthralled by the fact that I wore a tank top. I had on a rainbow necklace, rainbow earrings, and a black tank top that said Love Wins in rainbow letters. Before this day, I had never worn a tank top unless we were boating or swimming. Members of our church believed in modest clothing, which includes covering shoulders and wearing shorts and skirts that extend to the knee. I wore that type of clothing for twenty-five years, to Disney World in a hot and humid July and on hikes in ninety-degree sun. That constraint had never bothered me, but now I was ready to show the world that I did not follow those strict rules. It wasn't that I wanted to wear something different as much as the fact that I wanted to be allowed to, and I wanted to show others that I wasn't in that club anymore.

Because of Covid, the Pride month organizers held a march rather than a parade, which was disappointing in some ways but also more fun in others. First, we gathered on the lawn of the capitol building and listened to inspirational speakers. Unfortunately, the sound quality was low, so we didn't catch all the messages, but we clapped and cheered at the appropriate times. After that, we marched downhill about twenty blocks to a park filled with booths and tents featuring displays that highlighted and celebrated the LGBTQ experience. A giant rainbow balloon arch led the way for the marchers. The crowds were huge—when I turned around to look, it seemed like an endless wave of brightly colored clothing and rainbows. It was thrilling to see so many people who felt strongly about LGBTQ rights and needs. Smiling at others in the crowd and knowing that we were in this together filled me with a sense of community and purpose. It was an amazing moment in time.

A few days later, we left for a family vacation to Hawaii. We had planned this trip in January, with faith that Covid restrictions would lift and we'd be allowed to travel by then. When Haley came home, we got her a ticket on our flights and added her onto the different activities. I was glad to have another distraction for Haley, although her trip to Lake Powell had not gone well. She was miserable there, continually ruminating on the fact that she has lost her confidence and energy. Irrational thoughts ran through her mind such as: no one wants me here; they are being kind out of pity, but they don't really like me. She compared her current experience with how Lake Powell had been the previous summer and became even more depressed. She cried a lot and separated herself from the others when she could. When she was out on the houseboat, there was no cell service, but when they came into the marina, she called me in distress. I tried to help her, but I wasn't sure what to say. I knew that pointing out the illogic of her thoughts wouldn't help. I was shocked that this malady of the mind had such a firm hold on her. It was not going to be easy to reduce or detach it.

Considering her experience in Lake Powell, I knew Hawaii wouldn't be a cure-all for Haley. But at least it was something, and it gave me the opportunity to stay with her and observe her daily. It was a struggle to do that, though. She would hang back when we walked somewhere, stay reserved and quiet in family discussions, and say she'd rather stay in her hotel room than come out to the beach. One day, I came up to her room to check on her and found her sobbing. She had watched a docuseries on the Central Park Five and was overcome with despair and grief. She cared deeply about social justice issues and was greatly affected by the instances of inequality and prejudice in America. I commended her dedication to the cause but suggested that she not watch anymore of those shows until she was more emotionally stable.

Our family often talks about politics, current events, and social justice problems when we're together. Kaitlin is usually the one to get these conversations started, and she has a lot to say about them. Topics such as colonialism, misogyny and feminism, and the dynamics of white supremacy in America come up almost every time we're gathered. This is one of the reasons Haley hesitated to join in family conversations. Not only did these discussions discourage her, but also, she felt like she wasn't as smart or as informed as other members of the family. But when she and I spoke alone, she expressed great passion for these causes. Most of the church members she interacted with on her mission were politically conservative, and she became increasingly frustrated with their opinions, which she saw as outdated and harmful. Having LGBTQ siblings made her more sensitive to instances of inequality and discrimination, not to mention outright hateful behavior.

I could tell Haley felt frustration toward the church and its homophobic and racist policies and actions. Bryan and I leaned liberal in our politics, but she jumped all the way in. She had conveyed other irritations about the church as well. She resented the many rules and expectations required on her mission and how she felt she could never live up to them. Missionaries were encouraged to make goals frequently and in multiple capacities. Monthly goals, roommate goals, goals about bringing people to church, mission goals—it seemed to Haley that it never ended and that she wasn't competent enough to accomplish what was required in the different areas. To her, the structure of the mission created feelings of inadequacy and crushing despair. Once she got home, her antipathy extended to the church in general. She confessed to me one day that she dreamed about making a list of all the rules of the church and purposely trying to break each one.

I realized as we discussed these topics that she would probably not stay in the church and would not be distressed if I announced my departure. I still wasn't sure how or when to tell the kids, though. Fortunately, it came up naturally while we were in Hawaii. We stayed at the Hilton Hawaiian Village in Waikiki for a few nights and then went over to the Marriott in Ko Olina. We played on the beach, went snorkeling at Hanauma Bay, and took a catamaran boat tour to see dolphins and snorkel some more. Oahu was as beautiful as I remembered. It lived up to the expectations we had set for the kids. I was thrilled to show them the places and activities that Bryan and I had experienced more than ten years before.

We were not the only ones who had the idea to travel again once the Covid restrictions let up, however. Everywhere we went was packed. It took over two hours to get out of the airport because of the lines for checking Covid tests. There were giant crowds at the pools and island attractions. The hotels and restaurants had not rehired the staff they needed to perform at capacity levels, or if they had hired them, they weren't adequately trained. The result was long waits at hotel check-ins and at restaurants. It took patience and perseverance to get employees' help or service. I tried to reframe it into an opportunity to practice serenity, and we ended up having a great time despite these inconveniences.

One hot and slightly windy day, we spent time on the beach at our hotel in Waikiki. The sun climbed up the clear blue sky until it shone from the very center. We had lounge chairs by the pool and from there we could see the glistening ocean. Majestic palm trees lined the pathway to the beach, and under them stood bushes with dark green waxy leaves and bright pink flowers. The grassy areas on either side of the pathway were almost electric-green. It was relaxing and revitalizing to sit next to the pool and enjoy the view.

At one point in the afternoon, Haley and I ended up in the ocean together. The water was calm, with subtle waves coming in at intervals. We stood about waist deep and bounced around, walking back and forth. The sun's reflection in the water made the sandy bottom look like it held diamonds. The tan floor gave way to turquoise and then navy-blue water as you gazed out to the horizon.

Haley hadn't been talkative that day, but at least she was down at the beach with us. Once we were on our own, she opened up more. She said, "I like your swimsuit, but I've never seen you wear a bikini." It was true. Along with no tank tops, my rules of modesty included only wearing one-piece swimsuits, although in recent years I had worn "tankinis"—two-piece suits that still cover the midsection. In the past, I told myself that I didn't want to show my imperfect stomach anyway, but on this trip, I discovered that bikinis are more comfortable. Less material clinging to my skin was worth the potential embarrassment of showing my rounded and bulgy stomach.

Haley looked at me with interest, waiting for my reply. "Yes," I said. "This is my first time wearing a bikini, and it feels great!" She narrowed her eyes with suspicion and continued questioning me. "Also, I noticed that you let Sydney watch R-rated movies now," she challenged. When she and the others were teens, they were only allowed to watch PG-13 movies. "What has changed? Why are the rules different?"

I took a moment to collect my thoughts. It seemed disingenuous to brush off her inquiries. I decided now was as good a time as any to get into it. "That's a good question, and I'm not surprised you've noticed a difference. Dad and I have decided that the rules of the church are too restrictive and often feel arbitrary. We aren't going to hold ourselves or you kids to that standard anymore. We want to decide for ourselves what rules are appropriate for our family. In fact, I am going to stop going to church and not be a part of Christianity anymore."

Haley's eyes widened slightly, and she nodded slowly. "Wow. That's huge."

"I know. I've been wanting to tell you, but I needed to see where you were at with the church first. I worried that this admission might be upsetting and throw off your mental health and wellness. I have felt like this for a while, so it was somewhat difficult to be supportive of your mission, but I tried my best. How do you feel about it?"

"I'm fine with your leaving," she began. "I'm thankful that you guys supported me on my mission and didn't feel upset or disappointed when I came home. I know many parents wouldn't have responded that way. I don't know what I'll do in the long run, but right now I'm also ready for a break from the church.

"What made you decide to leave now?" Haley asked, "Is it because of Brooke and the LGBTQ policies of the church?"

"Kind of," I answered. "But that was only the final straw. I have felt uncomfortable with parts of the church for quite some time. I don't like the idea of missionary work, with its emphasis on insisting people come to church, get baptized, and commit to obedience. And I hesitated to persuade those who left the church to come back. That rubs me the wrong way. It feels manipulative and condescending, like, 'Let me show you the *right* way to live.' I want to allow people to do what they want to do; I don't want to coerce them into something different from that. I know Christians see missionary work as bringing hope and knowledge to the unknowing and unbelieving, but in practice, it feels icky.

"There are two other big reasons I'm ready to be done with religion. First, I have learned through life coaching that different ways of living aren't better or worse, they just are. We create a story about them, and that story helps us feel better about the way we choose to live. But then we use the story to judge and persecute others. I'm done with that whole paradigm.

"The other reason is that white supremacy is closely tied to Christianity. Once my eyes were opened to that, I couldn't remain part of the faith any longer. The culture of Christianity is white culture, and we tout it as the righteous way and the only way to heaven. The propagation of that philosophy has contributed greatly to the unjust society we live in. Because Christianity is entangled with colonization, misogyny, genocide, and white supremacy, I have a hard time believing it's true anymore.

"Christianity is narrow-minded, preaching that there is only one way to live. It's important to me to value all people and all of humanity, to learn from other people and understand their experiences. Christianity isn't about listening and learning from others; it's about convincing others to be like us. This 'I'm good/you're bad' structure they set up is harmful. It feels nice to the 'good' people but justifies horrible behavior toward those who don't look or act like you."

I told Haley about how I believe that everyone is doing his or her best, and how if that's true, a heaven or hell in the afterlife doesn't make sense. I told her how I have started to value letting people have their self-expression, not having so many rules and restrictions on behavior, and accepting and loving people as they are. She nodded in agreement at that. I said Christianity teaches that members should love and accept people, but the organization it sets up doesn't lend itself to that. It's hard to accept and love people when you condemn their behavior and you're afraid that you or your loved one might act like them. I also explained my thoughts on religion versus spirituality and how the descriptions of the second were more aligned with my values right now.

"And then when Brooke came out," I said, "I was forced to face the church's LGBTQ policies, and, as we know, that wasn't pretty. It is appalling that they don't support gay marriage and won't permit gay people to participate in the rites and rituals that they say are required for entry to heaven. And they don't have the language or capacity to incorporate transgender people, including non-binary. LGBTQ people in the church go through life thinking they are a mistake, sinful, and not acceptable before God. Any religion that allows children, youth, or even adults to believe that is not right. It's harmful and offensive. I've always been uncomfortable with that doctrine, but now that it's close to our family, I outright reject it. I don't want to be a part of a church that teaches that. That doctrine not only affects members of the church, but also contributes to the discrimination and poor treatment of LGBTQ people in society at large."

I was so passionate about what I was saying I was almost out of breath. Haley was listening with fascination. I took a break and smiled. Haley gave a nervous laugh. I knew this surprised her and was not what she expected me to say. I'd been thinking these things for years but never vocalized them to my kids for fear that it would make them lose their faith.

"I don't want to go on and on," I continued, "but I want to end with this: I am glad that Brooke is who they are and that they came out to us this year. I'm glad they felt comfortable telling us, and I'm thankful we could be open-minded enough to support and love them. In truth, I feel blessed and joyful to be part of the LGBTQ community. The people there are loving, accepting, open, and vulnerable. White affluent Christians are closed off. They try so hard to be who and what they're supposed to be that their lives are constricted. I think many people feel that way in Christianity—that they can't be their true selves or get to know other people in an authentic way. I'm glad to be done with that posturing and to be able to relax, be real, and be true to my inner thoughts and feelings. Letting go of the expectations and doctrines of the church has felt so freeing."

"That makes sense," Haley said. "It sounds like you've thought about this a lot." Haley seemed dazed. I'm sure it was a lot to take in at once. We looked out at the ocean for a minute, each lost in our own thoughts. We talked more about it and eventually went up to the pool and joined the others.

That night after dinner, the kids came back to Bryan's and my hotel room. The large room had plenty of seating. In addition to the king bed, there was a desk and chair, a couch, and a side chair. Everyone found a place to sit. Some of them chatted about the delicious food at dinner, and others looked at their phones. I didn't want Haley to be the only one who knew my feelings about the church, so I decided to take this chance to talk to them all at once.

"You guys," I began, "Haley and I were talking in the ocean today, and something came up that I wanted to tell all of you." The kids perked up. They put their phones away and looked at me attentively. "I am not going to attend church anymore. I'm taking a break from church, from Christianity in general," I said. They nodded but looked like they wanted to know more. I briefly went over the factors that I had explained to Haley earlier.

Kaitlin, not surprisingly, was the first of the kids to speak. She said, "I have been wondering if you might say this. In our conversations over the last few months, I could tell you were struggling to stay committed to the teachings and culture of the church, understandably so. You guys know I'm having trouble staying, also. I'm not sure what I'm going to do, but I definitely agree with your reasons and thoughts."

Brooke spoke next, "I think everyone is aware that I'm not interested in the church, or in religion generally. I never have been. From the time I was young, I had doubts about the teachings and knew I probably wouldn't stay with the church once I was an adult. When they would teach their homophobic doctrines, I wasn't offended or hurt because I would think, 'They're wrong about that; this isn't true.'"

Haley had a question for Bryan, "Dad, what do you think? Will you keep going?"

Bryan shifted in his seat and a grimace briefly crossed his face. "I don't know," he said slowly. "I agree with what Mom said. The church's LGBTQ policies bother me. But, as you know, I'm in this leadership position right now. I enjoy serving and helping the congregation, and I feel like I should keep going for now. Plus, the church has brought a lot of good into my life over the years, including success at work and in relationships. I still think being involved in the church has benefits."

"What do you think about this, Sydney?" I asked, "Are you doing okay?" As usual, she didn't have much to say.

"I'm fine. I like going to church sometimes, but it's kind of boring. It is not a problem for me if you stop going."

"Okay, I'm glad," I responded. "As you guys know, we are more open about our feelings and difficulties now. I'm thankful for that and grateful for what we've been through in this past year and how our family has grown and become closer. So, if you have any further thoughts or concerns about this, let me know and we can discuss it."

After that, the conversation turned to other topics. We discussed the recent news that the Senate voted to make Juneteenth a national holiday. As we discussed how this was a good move forward but not enough in the fight for racial justice, I glanced over at Haley, wondering what thoughts and emotions brewed inside her. After a bit, she said she wanted to go to bed. The conversation ended, and the kids went to their rooms for the night.

I felt relieved that the kids now knew my truth. Going forward, I could be open about my thoughts, and I had no obligation to go to church. I planned to ask the president of the women's organization to find a replacement for me as her counselor. She was a friend of mine, so I knew she'd want to know more about my decision, and I felt comfortable talking to her about it. Often, when people leave religion, especially our strict sect, they feel guilty and worry what others will think. I did not have any of that emotion. I was confident in my decision and ready to explain it to anyone.

Part of the reason I felt comfortable making this decision is because I wouldn't be upsetting my parents or extended family. Most people in our church have many siblings, aunts, uncles, and cousins in the faith. One of the strengths of our church is the closeness it brings to families, but that can be a weakness when a family member wants to step away. Those who leave worry their family will feel disappointed in them. It can feel like separating from the church means separating from your family. Again, the irony of misdirected human desires isn't lost on me. I wished for many years my parents were religious and in the church with me, and now the fact that they weren't made my life easier.

My only minor worry had been the confusion my decision might cause my kids. During their formative years, we were entirely committed to the church and its teachings. As devoted members, we were steadfast in our habits of attending church on Sunday, holding family scriptures and prayer, and requiring the kids to participate in church activities. My new views about religion might lead me to feel regret or think we did something wrong in our parenting. Luckily, I had learned from life coaching that there are no mistakes. Whatever happened was supposed to happen. Believing that frees you from negative emotion and needless railing against the past.

Even if it was a "mistake" and the kids were upset about how we raised them in the church, that is how parenting goes. Children are humans with brains wired to look for problems and reasons outside of them for their negative emotion. Imagining that parents should be perfect is irrational, but also it reveals an underlying belief that kids aren't supposed to struggle or have any hardship. Liz helped me understand that it's okay for kids to experience negative emotion. We try to do our best as parents, but we will always be 50 percent great and 50 percent a mess, no matter how hard we try. When you accept that and reduce the self-criticism, you operate from positive emotion and do a better job of parenting. I choose not to regret living the church principles and teaching my children about them. There is no upside to regret. I'm going to move forward with the knowledge and experience I have now.

It was easy for me to leave not only because I had no regrets and no family who would be hurt, but also because leaving validated the creeping doubts I had all along. My actions now aligned with my inner being. I had heard the voice of my parents inside my head for so many years telling me religion was naïve and cringy, and now I could agree with that voice and therefore silence its pestering. Soon after I stopped going to church, I felt like someone utterly different. I was confused that anyone would even expect me to go. I knew this was my true self, my authentic self, and wondered how anyone saw me as a religious person.

The next month, July, we took the kids on another trip to Lake Powell. I felt uneasy as we prepared to go, remembering what happened the previous year on the day we left and what had occurred in the months following. It seemed unreal, what we had been through. It's like when you look back on the first few months of having a newborn. You shake your head in wonder and feel like it was a dream. Some might say it had been an incredibly hard year, but I was struck by the growth and amazing benefits we'd seen from these experiences. I'd gained a clarity and an authenticity I did not think possible.

Amanda couldn't come this year, so it was just the seven of us. We stayed in a hotel again and went down to our rented boat each day. The blue water contrasting with the red rock cliffs was as breathtaking as it was the year before. There was something about this place that lured you back year after year. We drove the boat through narrow canyons and wide-open bays. We took turns surfing and wakeboarding.

I wore my bikini and reveled in the comfort. The kids weren't as surprised this time. Sydney and Brooke also wore bikinis, which had been forbidden for Kaitlin and Haley when they were that age. Kaitlin complimented Sydney's suit, and Sydney replied, "Thanks!" Then she summed up our family's last year perfectly, "The rules keep getting fewer and the swimsuits smaller!" We all laughed at that.

One day we stopped in a bay to swim and cliff jump. Brooke was not interested in jumping, and neither was I. Instead, we brought the wake surfboard into the water, and we held onto it to stay afloat while we swam around. The water was very clear; we could see our legs kicking deep below us. When we initially jumped in from the boat, the water cooled us off slightly from the hot summer sun but was warm enough to stay in for a long time. As we floated around, we talked about why cliff jumping is lame, and things we like and dislike about boating. The conversation turned to the future, and Brooke spoke with hope and optimism regarding the coming school year. They would be a senior in a few weeks and looked forward to applying to college. I asked what they might study at college, and they bubbled with enthusiasm. "There are so many fields I'm interested in," they said. "I love art, but I don't think I want to major in that. I like science. I think I might want to major in chemistry!"

It astonished me to contemplate the difference between the two trips. Eleven months before, Brooke had been reserved and dispirited. At that time, I was filled with worry and anxiety about their mental health and what the future would hold for them. Now they were animated and hopeful about school and college and life. I was amazed and relieved.

Haley wasn't in the same place, unfortunately. But I trusted that it would all be okay. I could be the hero of the story and not the victim. I was watching the movie of her life and believed it would have a happy ending eventually. I could handle whatever problems came our way and whatever negative emotion I created for myself. This is what it's like to be human.

The dream of me, Bryan, and the kids staying happily active in the church forever was just that: a dream. Once I saw its ephemeral quality, I opened my grip and let it go. I could not have predicted or imagined the clarity and authenticity that came once I did.

THE END

APPENDIX 1

THE FACTORS

As I mentioned in the book, over the past few years I kept a list which eventually became 'The Factors' in my departure from religion. This list contained reasons Christianity didn't make sense to me and ways it is harmful to others. As the list got longer, I felt more uneasiness with my involvement in the church. When Brooke came out, the balance was tipped, and I had more reasons to leave religion than I had to stay.

1. "White Christian churches are anchor points for **white supremacy** in our society," Robert P. Jones states in *White Too Long: The Legacy of White Supremacy in American Christianity.* He continues: "Without white evangelicals, the primary issue that has rent the soul of America since the

beginning, the struggle for racial equality and justice, would suddenly become much more manageable."

I care deeply about racial issues in America. When I heard this statement and his further explanation on a podcast, I knew that he was right, and I knew that I could not feel good about being a part of that institution any longer.

2. The Christian **doctrines regarding LGBTQ people** are offensive and harmful. Not only do those policies cause emotional injuries, but they don't make sense. The church says all these people, upwards of 3–5% of the population, can't be part of salvation. It also doesn't make sense to demand that gay members be celibate to achieve exaltation. This means they can't hold hands, hug, have a life partner, love, and be loved. Most of us could not do that. Even if they could manage to be celibate, when they participate in church, they continually receive the message that they're wrong and sinful. Lastly, beyond hurting LGBTQ members of the church, these policies and practices contribute to the discrimination and bad treatment of LGTBQ people in society at large.

3. Christianity is **narrow-minded**, believing that there is only one way to live (and the right way is heavily influenced by white culture). It's based in fear and creates worry that you or your kids might not live that one way and, consequently, might not make it to heaven. That distress hinders happiness and peace—virtues that, ironically, Christianity claims to generate.

4. The **guilt and shame** created from church standards are unnecessary and unhelpful. The obligations and burdens of

believing that we "should" do certain things is detrimental to our mental health. Religion's emphasis on guilt compounds our natural tendency toward self-criticism and creates unhappiness. When I realized that self-compassion and acceptance are more powerful motivators than judgment, I thought, "Why do we not learn this in the scriptures?!"

5. Christianity isn't about listening and learning from others. It's about **convincing others** to think and act like "us." I value all people and all of humanity. I want to learn from people different from me and understand their experiences.

6. Christianity is too entangled with **colonization, white supremacy (see #1), genocide, and misogyny**. Western European Christians set out to save the world by taking possession of other countries, exploiting their resources, spreading diseases, and killing whoever was in the way. Additionally, they preached that women were subservient to and, for many centuries, the property of men. Believing that God is male and that only males can direct the church and communicate with God inevitably leads to fundamental sexism.

7. The **"I'm good/you're bad" structure** Christianity sets up is harmful. It feels pleasant to the "good" people but justifies horrible behavior toward those who don't look or act like you. This dynamic plays into numbers 5 and 6 above.

8. I believe that every person is doing his or her best, so how can there be a **post mortal judgment** where people are assigned to heaven or hell?

9. I value letting people have their self-expression, which means not having so many **rules and restrictions on behavior and appearance**. These rules lead to judgment of others.

10. Believing you have the **"one way to heaven"** is egocentric. We live in a huge world full of billions of people, yet it's difficult for the human mind to comprehend that. It's easier to make assumptions and hold beliefs based on the few thousand people around you. I somehow gained the wider perspective and then found it difficult to believe that these doctrines and ordinances were the only way to salvation or exaltation, and we were the only ones who knew about them. Even as a practicing member, I was not fully convinced that my family members outside the church had no chance at going to heaven.

11. Christian doctrine teaches that members should love and accept everyone, but its other teachings don't lend themselves to that. It's **hard to accept and love people** when you condemn their behavior and fear you or your loved ones acting like them.

12. **Every group believes they're the best**, the most honest, that their way of life is best and just a little better than the others. Social psychology studies have unveiled this pattern in human behavior. When you know that, you realize you're not better. We're not as unique as our religious leaders say we are.

13. When I interacted with people in the LGBTQ community, I saw how loving and accepting they are. They are open and vulnerable. White affluent Christians are **closed off** and trying so hard to be who and what they're supposed to be. They don't want to show any weakness, and they compare themselves to

others to make sure they're doing a good enough job. I think many Christians feel like they can't be their true selves.

14. **The light half/dark half**. My experiences in the church were mostly positive. The teachings and practices of the church benefited me and my family, and I saw others in my congregation who worked hard to be good people and to help others. But I realized that I was facing what I call the "light half," and behind me there was a "dark half." The dark half consists of the pain and harm caused by these same teachings and practices. These injuries commonly happen to marginalized groups but can also be felt by people who experience suffocation by the endless demands of the church and believe they are never enough or that God disapproves of them and doesn't love them. Once I recognized that dark half, I couldn't in good conscious turn back to the light half and forget about the wounds afflicting other people.

15. I've always been uncomfortable with **reactivation** (trying to get people who stopped attending church to come back) **and missionary work**. I knew it annoyed my parents and brothers when church members visited or dropped off treats. My general world view is that we should let others do what they want and not try to coerce them or be manipulative. When these tasks were part of my leadership responsibilities, I had to push myself to care whether people came to church or not.

16. I've had **the "voice" of my family** in my head for many years saying that religious people are naïve, silly, and cringey.

17. I don't want to be religious if **my kids aren't**. I didn't like the separation from my family of origin because of our

different views on religion. I looked forward to having my husband and kids with me at church. When our kids started leaving, it wasn't worth staying and being, once again, the silly and naïve one. I didn't want to be disapproving of them or their choices. Some people can stay in the church and still feel unrestricted love and acceptance toward their inactive kids, but it didn't feel possible for me.

18. **Satan**. I've always thought that it was a weird concept to believe that there is an otherworldly being who continually tries to get you to do bad things. I could see that this concept was created to scare people and control their behavior. It wasn't logical to me, and as an active member, I tried not to think about it.

19. It has been said that to find congruency in your own life, to feel settled and harmonious with who you are, you have to first go through the inward process of learning who you are and embracing yourself. Then you must **live authentically**, which is the outward expression of what you've learned about yourself. I don't want to pretend anymore or come across as someone who cares about religious or scriptural conversations. I want to talk about abortion rights and the death penalty and Biden's awesome infrastructure bill. Those are things that I'm interested in, and I want to be authentic in that. I want to have people know that side of me, the real me.

APPENDIX 2

RELIGION HAS ITS BENEFITS

As you mature and gain critical thinking skills, you realize that life is complicated. Things are not black and white; there is always a context to consider. Some people who leave religion want to vilify it and claim it was the root of all their problems. However, I saw many aspects of religion that were useful and beneficial to me. As I stepped away, I tried not to throw the proverbial baby out with the bathwater. I focused on the good things that came from my involvement with the church and felt grateful for them. Maintaining some of these practices with a secular perspective can continue to be valuable to me and my family.

Religious practice	Secular benefit
Prayer	Builds a practice of expressing gratitude and setting intentions.
Scripture study	Gives benefits similar to meditation.
Fasting once a month and keeping the Sabbath day holy	Periodic abstaining increases our appreciation and enjoyment of those activities.
Tithing	Separates us from our money and helps us realize it was never ours in the first place, we are simply the steward of it.
Weekly family meetings to teach the gospel and daily family devotionals (scripture study and prayer)	Provides structured family time. Some of our best family conversations happened during these devotionals. The conversations weren't church related necessarily, just topics that came up because we were spending time together—things that might not have been talked about otherwise.

Religious practice	Secular benefit
Youth standards	Prevents kids from high school drinking and sex. Having a religious reason can be more persuasive than simply asking them not to do those things.
Church on Sunday	Imparts a routine, dedicated family time, and a unity of beliefs.
Family history/learning about ancestors	Teaches kids where they come from. Understanding the hard situations our ancestors went through shows that we can accomplish great things too.
Congregation	Furnishes a community: people who care about us and whom we can care for.
Emphasis on relationships	Creates a culture of spending time together and working to strengthen family bonds.

Religious practice	Secular benefit
Opportunities to serve others, from daily acts of kindness to large group service projects	Generates positive feelings, reduces isolation, keeps things in perspective.
Youth groups	Provides kids with positive peer pressure and adult role models and mentors.
Stretching ourselves to serve in leadership roles	Allows us to prove to ourselves that we can accomplish more than we thought we could and that it always works out.

APPENDIX 3

WHY I DO NOT REGRET MY TIME IN THE CHURCH

There are many people who have had painful and harmful experiences in the church, whether with the doctrine or with individual people. I don't discount or dismiss their stories, but I never faced that myself. As you see in Appendix 2, I can identify many benefits to living a religious life. Additionally, I didn't feel looked down upon or treated less than because I am a woman. I was always treated with respect and kindness. I knew and still know many wonderful people in the church.

These people care about others and want to make the world a better place. They just do it in their own way.

Furthermore, my time in the church was unique because I chose it as a youth and continued to choose it throughout adulthood. I never felt obligated or manipulated into going. This obviously leads to a more positive outlook on the church.

But in general, I choose to believe that no one makes you do things. When you believe others made you stay in the church, or when you think of the past in terms of coercion and force, you lose your power. *You* chose to go; *you* chose to say yes to church responsibilities. That is empowering. You maybe didn't see the whole picture and wouldn't make the same choices today, but it was you and your choice, and that's okay. You did what you thought was best at the time. No one forced you.

I also believe that there is no waste of time. Some who leave the church regret the time they spent there. But it is also an option to think that you did everything the way you were supposed to; your life went just as it was supposed to go. There were lessons you or your family needed to learn from that experience. The idea that the involvement was a waste is just a story, and it causes pain when you hold on to it. The universe is always conspiring in your favor. It was always meant to be this way. Even if you can't identify any good things that came from your time in the church, you can trust that they exist, and you just can't see them right now—but you will one day.

Some people might have regrets about the way they parented their children (or the way they were parented) because of their membership in the church. I would definitely have done things differently knowing what I know now, but I don't mourn or regret the past. Any way you parented or were parented as a child was bound to be somewhat good and somewhat messed up. That's the way of human relationships. You can't avoid it. There's nothing particularly bad about a religious upbringing. It's just one of life's choices.

This point was driven home for me when I read an essay from a woman whose mother was a liberal women's rights activist. The daughter didn't write the essay to say, "I'm glad I wasn't raised in a strict religious household." She didn't say, "I'm thankful I felt free to pursue whatever I wanted." No. She said that, although she went to rallies and donated money to social justice causes, she was pained because she never did as much as her mother and felt like she didn't quite measure up. This is called being human.

Being mad at the church is a choice, and I choose not to be. Same with harboring regrets. I'm not perfect at creating positive emotions. I choose to be frustrated or disappointed with myself often and for irrational reasons. But I am blessed to be able to let go of anger quickly, to have that calm, flat feeling, and know that this is how it was supposed to go. It doesn't always make sense to our human minds and perspectives, but I choose to have "faith" that this is true.

RECOMMENDED RESOURCES

To learn more about the noetic sciences, see https://noetic.org/

To find a life coach who can help you examine and loosen the thoughts that create your painful stories, go to www.thelifecoachschool.com/directory

To learn more about the U-Curve of Happiness see https://www.theatlantic.com/magazine/archive/2014/12/the-real-roots-of-midlife-crisis/382235/

https://www.theguardian.com/lifeandstyle/2018/may/05/happiness-curve-life-gets-better-after-50-jonathan-rauch https://www.washingtonpost.com/news/wonk/wp/2017/08/24/under-50-you-still-havent-hit-rock-bottom-happiness-wise/

Achor, Shawn. 2011. *The Happiness Advantage: The Seven Principles that Fuel Success and Performance at Work.* New York: Virgin Books.

Burns, David D. 2000. *Feeling Good: The New Mood Therapy.* New York: HarperCollins.

Coates, Ta-Nehisi. 2015. *Between the World and Me.* New York: Spiegel & Grau.

———. 2014. "The Case for Reparations." *The Atlantic*, June.

Katie, Byron, and Stephen Mitchell. 2002. *Loving What Is: Four Questions That Can Change Your Life.* New York: Harmony Books.

Prejean, Sister Helen. 1994. *Dead Man Walking.* New York: Vintage Books.

Saad, Layla F. 2020. *Me and White Supremacy: Combat Racism, Change the World, and Become a Good Ancestor.* Naperville: Sourcebooks.

Schlitz, Marilyn Mandala, Cassandra Vieten, and Tina Amorok. 2008. *Living Deeply: The Art & Science of Transformation in Everyday Life.* Oakland: New Harbinger Publications.

ENDNOTES

1 Prejean, Sister Helen, *Dead Man Walking* (New York: Vintage Books, 1994).

2 Coates, Ta-Nehisi, Interview by Stephen Colbert, *The Colbert Report* (June 16, 2014).

3 ———, "The Case for Reparations." *The Atlantic*, June 2014.

4 ———, *Between the World and Me.* (New York: Spiegel & Grau, 2015) p 9.

5 Ibid., p 9.

6 Ibid., p 9.

7 Ibid., p 14.

8 Ibid., p 37.

9 Ibid., p 76.

10 Ibid., p 79.

11 *I Am Not Your Negro*. Directed by Raoul Peck. Performed by

Samuel L. Jackson, (2015).

12 Ibid.

13 Saad, Layla F., *Me and White Supremacy: Combat Racism, Change the World, and Become a Good Ancestor,* (Naperville: Sourcebooks, 2020).

14 *I Am Not Your Negro.* Directed by Raoul Peck. Performed by Samuel L. Jackson, (2015).

15 Demby, Gene, and Shereen Marisol Meraji. "The White Elephants in the Room." *Code Switch.* [Podcast Audio], Produced by NPR. (November 18, 2020). https://www.npr.org/2020/11/17/935910276/the-white-elephants-in-the-room

16 Burns, David D., 2000. *Feeling Good: The New Mood Therapy,* (New York: HarperCollins, 2000).

17 The Life Coach School www.thelifecoachschool.com/directory

18 Katie, Byron, and Stephen Mitchell, *Loving What Is: Four Questions That Can Change Your Life,* (New York: Harmony Books, 2002).

19 Neff, Kristin. n.d. *Self-Compassion.* https://self-compassion.org/the-three-elements-of-self-compassion-2/

20 Schlitz, Marilyn Mandala, Cassandra Vieten, and Tina Amorok, *Living Deeply: The Art & Science of Transformation in Everyday Life,* (Oakland: New Harbinger Publications, 2008) p 15.

21 n.d. *About: The Interconnected Nature of Reality,* https://noetic.org/about/noetic-sciences/

22 n.d. *Our Origins: A Shift in Perspective,* https://noetic.org/about/origins/

23 n.d. *About: Weaving Together Knowledge and Knowing.* https://noetic.org/about/

24 Vieten, Cassandra, *What Are Noetic Sciences?* May 10, 2011 https://www.psychologytoday.com/us/blog/consciousness-matters/201105/what-are-noetic-sciences-0

25 Ibid.

26 n.d. *About: Weaving Together Knowledge and Knowing.* https://noetic.org/about/

27 Achor, Shawn, *The Happiness Advantage:The Seven Principles that Fuel Success and Performance at Work.* (New York: Virgin Books, 2011) p 30.

28 Ibid., p 15.

29 Ibid., p 44-45.

30 Ibid., p 67.

31 Ibid., p 69-70.

32 Ibid., p 70-71.

33 Ibid., p 71. Emphasis in original.

34 Simons, Daniel, *Selective Attention Test.* March 10, 2010. https://www.youtube.com/watch?v=vJG698U2Mvo

35 Schlitz, Marilyn Mandala, Cassandra Vieten, and Tina Amorok, *Living Deeply: The Art & Science of Transformation in Everyday Life,* (Oakland: New Harbinger Publications, 2008) p 15.

36 Rilke, Rainer Maria, n.d. *quotes.net.* https://www.quotes.net/quote/5913

37 Vanzant, Iyanla, n.d. *quotefancy.* https://quotefancy.com/quote/833842/Iyanla-Vanzant-Religion-is-the-rules-regulations-ceremonies-and-rituals-developed-by-man

Made in United States
Troutdale, OR
11/06/2023

14357424R00176